A HANDBOOK IN BUSINESS MANAGEMENT

by
Jacob W. Chikuhwa

authorHOUSE®

AuthorHouse™
1663 Liberty Drive
Bloomington, IN 47403
www.authorhouse.com
Phone: 1-800-839-8640

Published by AuthorHouse 5/30/2013

ISBN: 978-1-4817-5623-5 (sc)
ISBN: 978-1-4817-5622-8 (hc)
ISBN: 978-1-4817-5639-6 (e)

Library of Congress Control Number: 2013909301

To the Unknown
Auditor

TABLE OF CONTENTS

TABLES AND FIGURES

PREFACE

The task of selecting headings to be included in any branch of science offers many difficulties: in the case of economics, it is closely linked on with finance and general business studies, with political economy as regards political science. In starting this book, I had intended to write something thoroughly elementary, on a level with the average Zimbabwean aspiring to go into business (sole traders, co-operators, etc.). As things have turned out, portions, particularly Part Two (2.3), Part Three (3.2), (3.3) are substantially harder than originally intended. In addition Appendix I: Data Computation Techniques, is intended for the budding financial controller (manager).

It should be admitted that business studies is closely associated with manpower management, business administration, accountancy, marketing, purchasing and supply, product control, business law and a host of other subjects.

I have chosen manpower development, accounting procedures and data processing with the intention and hope to attempt a middle-of-the-road analysis to include those overlapping developments in business studies. Traditional disciplines like accountancy frequently have unavoidable use in commerce and industry. And on the other hand, data processing, particularly electronic data processing is of current interest in business studies and analysis.

This book offers to the professional student a preliminary survey of the fields of manpower development, accountancy and electronic data processing; while the wider public, whose enlightened interest is the mainspring of social progress, may, I hope, find in its pages something to stimulate reflection upon those larger issues which must be determined, if at all, by the consensus of their opinion. In outlining such a survey, in collecting materials for such reflection, I am aware that I have attempted what has often been done before. But as knowledge and experience grow, and as the material atmosphere of an age changes, there is always room for another attempt, especially, perhaps, for one that presents the data of business studies, as they are presented here, from a practical point of view. In short, an author need apologise not for doing the thing again, but only for not doing it better.

This book is not a discussion of current affairs. Some readers confronted with it can hardly fail to regret that the writer has thrown little light, or at all events little direct light, on the grave economic difficulties with which our economies are at present confronted — or some other such cliché. Alas, I must leave them to their regret. An author is entitled to choose his own topics, and potential readers who prefer other topics have a very simple remedy.

I have carefully considered the criticism of the book which have come under my notice, and have adopted all those suggestions which could be taken up, so far as they did not contradict the plan on which this volume was drawn; some criticisms were mutually destructive, others were due to insufficient knowledge of the original perception on the part of the critic, whilst others advocated radical changes, which would have made this, not my book, but some other person's product.

A brief description of the complexities of economic and business affairs may be necessarily misleading, but I hope that this book is not more misleading than the average of such books. I would have liked to write something even simpler, but if one is to include some firm structure of theory as well as mere description of facts, it seems impossible to simplify economics much further. I am strongly of the opinion that without its theoretical structure, economics is a poor, flabby subject; it is the attempts to explain the immense complexity of the real world by logical theories (manpower, accounting and electronics) which provide the students with worthwhile intellectual exercise and excitement.

I am greatly indebted to my colleagues in the academia and those in high corporate positions — Dr N. Dhlembeu, Dr M. A. B. Mutiti, Mr E. Razemba, Mr A. J. Patsanza and Dr W. Pause — for their advice and criticism. I would like to give special thanks to the authors and compilers of the various books and handbooks, journal reports and newspaper articles which made my task easier.

INTRODUCTION

Economics exert a great impact in the society, Adam Smith, David Ricardo, Friedrich Engels, Karl Marx, Keynes and Lenin all had theoretical ideas on development of society. For man to live, he has to influence the environment in order to change it to suit his needs — economic needs, that is. Contemporary economists are usually wary about the "dwindling resources". We talk of the "scarcity" of the means to satisfy our demands and yet man has invented new products to replace those "dwindling resources". One can think of synthetic rubber, fibre glass and contemporary genetic engineering has produced fantastic results in the fields of medicine and agriculture.

Confronted with such dangers as Acquired Immune Deficiency Syndrome (AIDS), the "green house effect", man is busy devising ways and means to combat these problems. With the spiralling oil prices during the mid 1970's, man invented rigs to extract petroleum from the sea-bed and others have discovered that sugar-cane can be processed to produce some alcohol that can be blended with petroleum to produce petrol. Health researchers have discovered that a drug which inhibits the growth of cancer cells can also kill the parasite that causes malaria. When the research team used cancer chemotherapy drugs called kinase inhibitors to treat red blood cells infected with malaria, the parasite was stopped in its tracks. According to World Health Organisation statistics, this deadly disease infected around 225 million and killed nearly 800,000 people worldwide in 2009.

It is recognised that development is an on-going process. We often read about developed (industrialised) nations and developing (Third World) nations. The fact, though, is that all nations are developing. What may differentiate them are the stages in their development.

Economics has evolved into a number of diverse disciplines such as marketing, purchase and stock control, statistics and the traditional discipline such as accounting. In the 1980's we witnessed the emergence of Development Studies as another economic discipline. "A Handbook in Business Management" makes an endeavour to combine three different areas of specialisation, viz. organisation and manpower development, financial management and electronic data processing, and to show their interrelationships.

Jacob W. Chikuhwa

Therefore, the purpose of this book is to give the reader an insight into the way organisations emerge and grow, and the relationships between manpower management, financial management and management information systems (MIS). A concerted effort has been made to project how one area is an integral part of the other. For one to succeed in business operations, one has to have the basic knowledge in the three areas of specialisation covered.

Business organisation and management will hardly appear as a straight-forward concept to the non-economist. In certain cases, however, business management coincides with the concept of efficiency in the private enterprise, i.e. minimum production costs for a certain output, maximum profit and such economic laws as the law of diminishing returns, the law of supply and demand and so on. It may truly be said that what is good for an organisation (firm) like Volvo Svenska Bil AB, or Anglo-American Corporation is good for the country. But in some cases, the two concepts of *private enterprise* and *social welfare* do not coincide at all. This is liable to cause misunderstanding and even among those who are expected to observe efficiency on a national level (such as politicians and government agencies) cannot avoid confusing the two concepts.

In many countries, especially the underdeveloped, this is particularly conspicuous in the field of public transport; bus and railway communications are brought to a grinding halt owing to losses at the "firm" level even in instances where such measures can be shown to be a waste of resources from the point of view of society as a whole. The reason for this neglect is the lack of appreciation of the important role of the organisation: manpower management, on the one hand, and financial management, on the other.

Business management, coupled with the need for efficiency, is also misunderstood in another way and for a completely different reason. It is often alleged that strictly-business efficiency and profit in general are connected with exploitation and capitalist tendencies, and even incompatible with values such as "equity", "cultural standards", "healthy working environment", etc. On the contrary, acts aimed at achieving business efficiency and profitability can, in fact, be said to promote more such values. Strictly speaking, this is so because business efficiency involves an attempt to take into account all individuals' evaluations of all consequences of economic (business) acts, i.e. not only the direct or purely material consequences of such acts.

To many people, economics seems difficult, even obscure. The main reason for this impression turns out to be that the money or financial aspects of the matter tend to be confusing. The crucial economic aspects, however, are generally much easier to grasp if the "veil of money" is lifted and the problem is looked at in real terms. To help clarify this position, consider that a person has bought some planks for $5 each to make a wooden box and it later turns out that he did not need all of them. Although it is certainly correct to say that the planks did cost $5 each (and that an additional piece would cost that much) this does not normally indicate anything about the value of the remaining planks. The value is determined solely on the basis of the possible ways of using these planks that this person might now think of having considered all the alternatives, including that of reselling them, he may find that the best one, after all, is to burn them. In that case, if his son happens to be looking for something to play with, giving the planks to him would certainly not entail a real cost of $5 each (the purchase price), but only what they are considered to be worth as fuel.

A considerable part of economics and especially the analysis of business efficiency, is based on a so-called opportunity cost argument of this uncomplicated kind, i.e. on the value of the best alternative use of a given resource, be it an available commodity, skilled manpower, a piece of machinery, or an hour of work.

It is an unfortunate fact that the desire to spell out the details of a complex economic reality usually makes it difficult to see the scope of the simple principle just mentioned. In an attempt to present business organisation and to facilitate an overall view of the general problem of business efficiency (financial management), "A Hand-Book in Business Management" is made relatively brief and free from elaborate details. This approach is based on the belief that once a bird's eye perspective has been acquired of organisation and manpower management, business management, it will be easier — at least for the patient student and business executive — to scrutinise practical situations and understand the real-world environment.

Jacob W. Chikuhwa

In Part One, it is shown that a simple organisation structure with, among other units, personnel, finance and transport, can be created and in turn generate situations that are socially efficient in the sense that further changes which benefit both the individual and the organisation are possible. The vital property is the strategy set to merge social and technological parameters selected for the projected organisation. Once the *selection of the manpower* to operate the *acquired machinery* is completed, an all-out effort should be started to further develop their skills to increase *efficiency and productivity*.

Part Two looks at the financial assumptions behind the organisation and manpower recruited to run the organisation. It is shown that a lack of financial expertise and absence of phenomena such as proper accounting procedures, the ability to keep proper books of accounts, etc. may ruin a good business proposal. It is shown that a *management interested in efficiency and increasing returns in production* can neutralise or eliminate financial pitfalls, thus helping a dynamic organisation achieve its objectives. Regardless of the actual choice of objectives for business development, we can feel free to assume that the desired overall financial status will be one of maximum efficiency provided that certain stabilisation and income distribution goals have been met.

At the same time, the organisation may be interested in achieving one particular efficient state of affairs by correcting certain practical obstacles. Part Three shows that with an efficient data processing system, *it is possible to adjust the situation before it goes out of hand.* Moreover, management may be dissatisfied with the way the finances of the organisation behave even if they tend towards the desired state. There are recurring shortfalls in the form of short-term general material and manpower problems. Management information systems are therefore important for the purpose of *adjusting income distribution and combating tendencies towards general organisation inefficiency*. Given carefully structured data processing systems, a general method can be established for decision-making or policy-making in individual cases of manpower recruitment and development, investment projects, income distribution, etc. — a so-called cost-benefit analysis.

It was felt that the book would be incomplete without certain data computation techniques. For a corporate manager, it is important to be able to undertake operational research techniques to help top management to make sound policy decisions. An ability to calculate depreciation charges and to carry out *financial forecasting is essential for the proper running of a business concern.* Some typical organisation charts and flowchart symbols were also added in the book's Appendix. It is hoped that these will act as a guideline for those involved in organisation and manpower development, especially those mandated with job specification and description.

Lastly, a glossary was compiled with the intension not only to include words and terminologies used in this book, but to reach a wider audience involved in a business environment. In mind is a business executive with little or no knowledge in economics, e.g. one specialised in electrical engineering, civil engineering, mining, etc. An effort was made to include terminology generally used in capital and money markets and labour organisation and other factors of production.

This book is targeted at those studying economics and specialising in manpower economics, finance, computerised information systems as well as business executives and small 'start-up' entrepreneurs. The book will help business concerns get a close appreciation on how to set up computerised data processing systems and networks: centralised vs. distributed data processing and the concept of a database.

PART ONE

1. ORGANISATION AND MANPOWER MANAGEMENT

1.1 Organisation Structure

While in-the-flesh organisations tend to be more or less complex, in the abstract, they can be made to appear rather simple. It is, in fact, true that an organisation is nothing more than a collection of people grouped together around technology which is operated to transform inputs from its environment into marketable goods or services. Organisations inseparably intertwine people and processes into what is currently referred to as a "sociotechnical" system. People in organisations operate the technology, they run the process. But they in turn, as part of the process, have much of their behaviour determined by the system they operate.

The concept of structure employed here refers to the way in which departments or units are arranged within a system, the linkages established among these, and the wages in which positions are arranged within them. First, management establishes and modifies structure by the way in which it groups tasks into units. It may, for example, pull together related tasks around a given product or stage in the process. Secondly, management establishes structure by binding units or departments together with lines of authority, responsibility, communication and control. The choice made in each of these areas clearly affects the role and task of the manager. Each subordinate manager's role and behaviour are strongly affected by the manner in which his unit is tied to those with whom it must interact. The way in which information flows between or among such units, the individuals within the organisation to whom these units report, the manner in which their outputs are evaluated, etc, all influence managerial behaviour. The manager is not entirely controlled by the structure in which he operates but he is at least constrained by it.

Organisation structures should not be regarded as static. Like organisms, they change according to the prevailing environment

Organisation and Manpower Management

although care must be taken not to make radical changes that may lead to disruption in the production of goods and services.

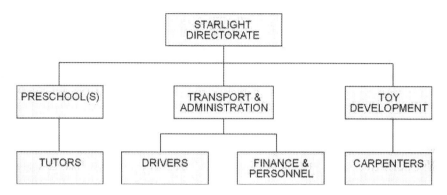

Fig. 1: Starlight Organisation Structure

Figure 1 above reflects two major "commodities" to be produced by Starlight. On the one hand are the toys and playground equipment required at a normal/standard preschool and on the other, are the services, i.e. the tutorship and the transport and administration that link the production of goods and services that make Starlight operative.

The structure further reflects the units and identifies more explicitly some of the variables that are associated with the organisation itself (the people and the technology they operate).

1.2 Organisation Variables

When we discuss organisations, we frequently feel the need to differentiate among them or to group them together along certain dimensions. Several such dimensions have been used, among the more prominent of which are goals and objectives, technology and manpower.

We readily so classify organisations according to their goals and objectives, — even in casual conversations. For example, we differentiate between product/service and output. Important differences appear to exist between a steel firm and an educational institute (although in this age of the conglomerate such differences seem to be disappearing), and we imply that a substantial gap does or should exist

Jacob W. Chikuhwa

between religious and brokerage houses though each may feel that it is engaged in the determining and disseminating of services.

Similarly, we differentiate among organisations according to their technology, or the methods they use to get things done. A housewife concerned about zoning regulations has a mental picture of the characteristics of light versus heavy industry, and most of us, from observation or imagination, can discuss such differences and some of their more dramatic implications — as, say, between an assembly plant and a research and development organisation.

Finally, we regularly refer to or distinguish between organisations in accordance with characteristics (specialisation) related to their manpower. We separate, and have feelings about, large and small organisations, and we differentiate impersonal, professional, nationally owned and operated firms from locally controlled ones, frequently stating or implying a value judgement as we do.

Starlight Goals and Objectives

The goals and objectives of organisations, in theory and in fact (though the fact is sometimes difficult to describe), result from interactions with the environment. In the public sector, the idealised process occurs as follows:
(a) society has a visible need,
(b) constituents demand that it be filled,
(c) legislators vote into existence an organisation to meet this need, i.e. by an Act of Parliament. Of course, examples can be pointed out where the process appears to have been reversed, or begun in the middle, but generally this procedure tends to hold. In the private sector, the process, though somewhat less visible, is similar.

It is logical to consider land and buildings as the first requirement for the establishment of Starlight. The term 'land' is used to describe all those natural resources over which man has power of disposal and which may be used to yield an income. It includes, therefore, farming and building land, forests, mineral deposits, fisheries, rivers, lakes — all those resources freely supplied by nature which man needs in producing the things he wants. The supply of building land has increasingly become limited. Economists have always emphasised this particular aspect of land and there is one very important application of the principle of fixed supply in the case of the site value of land, especially in urban areas. On the other hand, the cost of putting up buildings is dictated by the prevailing retail prices of construction materials.

Whatever his personal motives, the entrepreneur moves to provide a product or service which the public will purchase, with the purchase demonstrating a real or presumed need. This process is sanctioned directly by the granting of a corporate charter or business licence, and indirectly by our total economic-political system, which promotes privately controlled production of goods and services.

There appears to be a growing consensus, therefore, that in Zimbabwe the development of preschool institutions has been taken as a priority.

Starlight is envisaged as both a production and service concern. In the first place, it is to serve as a preschool educational institution where the following enrolment categories would be considered:

Age Group I	3 year to 4 year olds
Age Group II	4 year to 5 year olds
Age Group III	5 year to 6 year olds

Each age group would consist of a maximum of twenty-five (25) children.

Secondly, the concern would provide transport for the children enrolled at its institutions. In addition, it would be responsible for the transportation of materials, including food stuff, needed for the smooth running of the preschools. Materials needed for the repairs and development of toys used in the preschools would also be transported by the concern's own transport system. The transport system would be developed to provide services for the Starlight preschool employees and other inner-city commuters. The aforesaid two objectives entail the establishment of haulage and minibus and taxi systems.

Thirdly, Starlight would be engaged in the development and manufacture of toys. The finished products would be earmarked not only for the Starlight preschools, but for other preschools or nurseries. The initial stage would be to satisfy the Starlight preschools' demand before establishing retail outlets to stock any surpluses.

Directors/managers may find that their primary task is that of attempting to cope with changing environmental demands, adjusting organisational goals and objectives as rapidly as possible in order to

Jacob W. Chikuhwa

keep them aligned with the wishes of powerful constituents. Of course, even where the organisation is large and powerful, it generally finds it difficult to influence or maintain control over the demands of its environment completely and/or indefinitely. The most prestigious firms and governmental agencies have proved vulnerable to private and public muckrakers and pressure groups lie in wait to ambush the organisation's efforts to protect itself from environmental demands. There appears to be a growing consensus that the need for managerial skill in adjusting rapidly to, or controlling, environmental demands is becoming increasingly essential.

Starlight Management's continuing task of interpreting and making the concern's goals and objectives relevant and operational at all levels is obviously made easier when product/service and purpose are closely linked and the contribution of various activities to these throughout the concern is clearly visible.

Similarly, Starlight may discover that in some areas it is achieving its goals and objectives more effectively by serving as a source of employment opportunities than by giving tuition and producing toys.

Starlight Technology

The technology of an organisation includes not only the visible machinery, tools and equipment used in turning out its product or service, but also the specific human skills, knowledge and procedures used to operate these devices.

We can imagine various sets of continua on which we might classify and differentiate technologies. For example, we might array them from those built around simple, multipurpose hand tools to those that are highly specialised and almost completely automated. Or we might focus on the input and output ends of the process and arrange technologies in terms of the variability of the materials feeding in the complexity or the diversity of the products or services coming out.

Considering that we have derived a meaningful classification scheme in Starlight, that captured and highlighted the key variables among different technologies, we should then examine the impact of each class of category on management — on its role, attitudes and behaviour. A manager, of course, is not controlled by the organisation's technology, but its characteristics (specialisation) restrict the range of alternatives

Organisation and Manpower Management

open to him at any given moment. One of his key tasks is, of course, to operate a technology as effectively and as efficiently as possible, but an increasingly important requirement is that he be able to cope with change — to recognise the need for and to make adjustments in the technology to keep it aligned with organisational needs and environmental influences, and at the same time to adjust his own role and behaviour to match the changes in technology.

The equipment required to facilitate the smooth running of Starlight would include:

(a) preschool — a stove, a refrigerator, deep freezer, cooking utensils, plates and cutlery and furniture.

(b) transport — a minibus, preferably A Nissan Civic Diesel and a pickup truck (diesel).

(c) carpentry — a circular saw (major) and its accessories, an auto planer and its accessories.

It should be noted that working and productive capital accumulation together makes up the dominant component in the demand for finance in most concerns and consequently has to be trimmed to available finance, which, in turn, is composed of expected internal financing and borrowing. The basic factors determining investment goods demand are to be found among the factors determining the services and production planned.

Whenever the investment plans are elaborate in terms of project specifications — which is always the case in budgeting and usually the case in long-term planning — each project should be identified with a plan to e.g. expand capacity at a particular production line at one particular location and with elaborate technical specifications attached. After approval of the investment plan, an appropriation precedes each commitment to start spending on capital account. The appropriations plan or procedure is a matter of regular occurrence each month or more often and is carried out at several stages in the organisation's hierarchy.

In general, the investment plan and the appropriations plan (budget) are two different things. The investment plan is a solution to the comprehensive plan when all relevant factors have been taken into account. It defines how large a portion of total funds, expected to be available, that is planned to be allocated on capital account. It cannot be

Jacob W. Chikuhwa

determined until the financing side has been considered. The appropriations plan comes later and is designed to finalise the selection of individual projects within the so determined frame. It is final and means authority to start making commitments. Normally, however, some individual project specification takes place already in the making of the investment plan.

Starlight Manpower

Manpower resources comprise the total effective effort that can be put to work as shown by the number of people and hours of work available, the capacity of employees to the work and their productivity.

Starlight's initial manpower requirements would be: three (3) tutors, one (1) driver, one (1) bookkeeper, one (1) receptionist/typist, one (1) cook, one (1) cleaner, one (1) carpenter and one (1) general hand.

After having classified employees by function and/or department, occupation, level of skill and status planned, it is management's task to select the people required. Besides the skills or abilities, from the point of view of the preparation of management development programmes, it can be equally important to select people with potential for advancement. Selection of manpower by age helps to pre-empt problems arising from a sudden rush of retirements or a preponderance of older employees. Another factor which is equally important is the length of service with previous employers for this will provide evidence of survival rates, which are a necessary tool for use by management in predicting future resources.

When selecting manpower, management considers manpower productivity and costs to be significant. Manpower selection is just as concerned with getting the numbers required as making the best use of the people selected. Selection methods should be designed with an objective to employ people with high performance potential and those with greater scope for personal achievement and recognition, more challenging and responsible work; people with more opportunity for individual advancement and growth at the same time as the new Starlight concern grows.

Once manpower has been selected and employed, it is important that management should put an effort into their development. This is concerned with improving the performance of employees, giving them

Organisation and Manpower Management

opportunity for growth and development, and ensuring, so far as possible, that promotion within the organisation is provided for. The objectives of a typical *manpower development programme* can be defined as an endeavour to *improve the financial and long-term growth of the organisation* by:

(a) Improving the performance of employees by seeing that they are clearly informed of their responsibilities and by agreeing with them specific key objectives against which their performance will be regularly assessed.

(b) Identifying employees with further potential and ensuring that they receive the required development, training and experience to equip them for more senior posts within their own locations and divisions with the organisation.

1.3 The Role of Management and that of the Organisation

Setting up of a business concern does not end with the acquisition of land and buildings, plant and equipment and the recruitment of personnel to operate the technology. Immediately after setting up a business concern, the daunting process of development starts. It should be noted that development is an on-going process. Many an organisation have often grown from virtually back-yard and unknown concerns into giant conglomerates. One of the chief catalysts in the development of an organisation is management. The manager's chief task, as I perceive it, is that of integrating organisational and human variables into an effective and efficient sociotechnical system. On occasion, management carries out this task rationally and before the fact, attempting to blend an appropriate mix of these variables. More often, management finds that someone has already provided them with a recipe and that one of the sets of variables, organisational or human, is more or less fixed and they must adjust the other set to it. Typical here is the situation where goals and objectives and technology are set and the manager's task is that of fitting persons with an appropriate set of characteristics to them. On occasion, however, the opposite occurs — the manager has before him a group of people with given characteristics (specialisations) for whom he

Jacob W. Chikuhwa

must design appropriate objectives and a structure through which these can be accomplished. Figure 2 below gives a good illustration.

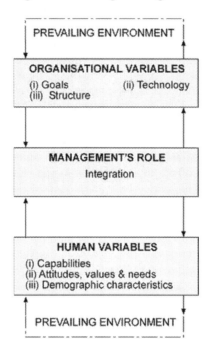

Fig. 2: Integration of Human and Organisational Variables

Most often, the manager finds himself in the midst of an on-going sociotechnical system, with concurrent — and frequently conflicting — requirements for adjustments of both organisational and human needs and characteristics. The manager is influenced and/or constrained by both organisational and human variables and, in turn, as having an impact on them, modifying and adjusting them in the interest of organisational performance.

Just like a technician or mechanic, the manager uses certain tools — integrative tools or a set of mechanisms. The following mechanisms are some of the more important means by which managers carry out their integrative task:

(i) <u>Direction</u>

Organisation and Manpower Management

The manager attempts to blend human attitudes and energies to achieve organisational objectives through the mechanism of direction, i.e. decision and policy making, supervision, etc. He explains these objectives, plans how they can be attained, issues instructions concerning how, when, and by who these plans will be carried out, and, in person or through reports, oversees their progress. With regard to this mechanism, managerial behaviour might range:

(a) from unilateral determination of plans, policies and objectives to joint determination with those individuals affected;

(b) from close and direct supervision (either in person or through detailed procedures and reports) to general, supportive supervision which allows broad self-direction and self-control to be exercised in the pursuit of agreed-upon objectives.

(ii) Organisation and Job Design

Here the manager attempts to merge people and technology into a smooth functioning system by structuring and restructuring organisational units and the jobs which make up these units. Alternatives available in utilising these mechanisms might range:

(a) from structures which arrange groups of functional specialists in traditional hierarchical layers to more loosely linked, self-paced teams with heterogeneous skills grouped around a product, part, service, or integrated stage of the process;

(b) from job designs emphasising highly specialised and segmented collection of tasks to designs which attempt to encompass a meaningful range of activities into self-paced, self-evaluated operations.

(iii) Selection and Training — Appraisal and Development

On an on-going basis, the manager uses selection and training devices to find and hire people with characteristics appropriate to organisational needs, and, once the individuals are in the organisation, he uses appraisal and development mechanisms to maintain and enhance these characteristics. For these mechanisms, alternatives might range:

(a) from selection and training processes which focus on presumed traits and abilities associated with immediate job requirements to more flexible systems which attempt to balance the long-term needs of the organisation and the individual;

Jacob W. Chikuhwa

(b) from superior-conducted appraisal based on standard characteristics and behaviour to joint appraisal (superior/subordinates) focused on progress toward previously agreed upon job targets or objectives.

(c) From unilaterally planned and directed development programs to flexible procedures where organisation members are included in the process of setting their own development goals and choosing the means of achieving them.

(iv) Communication and Control

The manager builds linkages between the technical system and its human element and between segments of the sociotechnical system through communication and control systems. Here alternatives might range:

(a) from communication systems which primarily provide for downward flows of orders and instructions and upward flows of reports to information systems designed to provide operating units with access to all the data they feel are necessary to their performance;

(b) control systems which collect progress information from operating units for transmission to distant evaluation points to short feedback loop designs which allow operating units to immediately appraise and adjust their own performance.

(v) Reward System

Finally, the manager uses a reward system to attract individuals to the organisation, maintain them within the system, and, hopefully, increase their performance level and contribution to the organisation. Within reward systems, alternatives might range:

(a) from systems built exclusively around either longevity or merit alone to more flexible systems which acknowledge both loyalty and performance;

(b) from unilateral determination of rewards and the method of their attainment to systems in which organisation members have a voice in determining the nature of rewards and the paths by which these can be achieved.

It should be acknowledged that while we have listed and described these mechanisms separately, they are in fact and in practice closely intertwined. They are all in operation, manifestly or latently, at the same time and what the manager does with regard to one of them affects what can and will be done with another. Unfortunately, many managers behave as if these mechanisms were separate and distinct and therefore fail, apparently, to recognise that what the one hand is accomplishing with adjustments to one mechanism, the other hand may be undoing with its adjustments to another.

It should not be overlooked that while managers are engaged in the activities to blend human attitudes and energies together with the organisation technology to achieve organisational objectives, they themselves need development. The traditional view is that the organisation need not concern itself with management development. The natural process of selection and the pressure of competition will ensure the survival of the fittest.

On the other hand, management development is seen mainly as a mechanical process using management inventories, multi-coloured replacement charts, 'Cook's Tours' for newly recruited graduates, detailed job rotation programs, elaborate points schemes to appraise personal characteristics, and endless series of formal courses.

The true role of the organisation in management development lies somewhere between these two extremes. On the one hand it is not enough, in conditions of rapid growth (when they exist) and change, to leave everything to chance — to trial and error. On the other hand, elaborate management development programs cannot successfully be imposed on the organisation. Because development is always self-development, nothing could be more absurd than for the enterprise to assume responsibility for the development of a man. The responsibility rests with the individual, his abilities, his efforts and his creative foresight. Every manager in business has the opportunity to encourage individual self-development or to stifle it, to direct it or to misdirect it. He should be specifically assigned the responsibility for helping all men working with him to focus, direct and apply their self-development efforts productively. And every company can provide systematic development challenges to its managers.

Executive ability is eventually something which the individual must develop for himself on the job. But he will do this better if he is given

Jacob W. Chikuhwa

encouragement, guidance and opportunities by his company and his manager. The role of the company is to provide conditions favourable to faster growth. And these conditions are very much part of the environment (Fig. 2) and organisation climate of the company and the management style of the chief executive who has the ultimate responsibility for management development.

Management development is not a separate activity to be handed over to a specialist and forgotten or ignored. The success of a management development program depends upon the degree to which all levels of management are committed to it. The development of subordinates must be recognised as a natural and essential part of any manager's job. But the lead must come from the top.

1.4 Management Development Activities

The management development activities required will depend on the organisation, on the one hand, its goals, its technology, its structure and philosophy and on the other hand, its human resources capabilities, attitudes, values and needs and demographic characteristics. (See Fig. 2) A bureaucratic, mechanistic type of organisation, such as a large government department, a nationalised industry, a major insurance firm or a large process manufacturing company, will be inclined to adopt the programmed routine approach, complete with a wide range of courses, inventories, replacement charts, career plans and management-by-objectives based review systems. An innovative and organic type of organisation may rightly dispense with all these mechanisms. Its approach should be to provide its managers with the opportunities, challenge and guidance they require, relying mainly on seizing the chance to give people extra responsibilities, and ensuring that they receive the coaching and encouragement they need. There may be no replacement charts, inventories or formal appraisal schemes, but people know how they stand, where they can go and how to get there.

Management development activities can be divided into seven areas:
　　(i)　　Organisation Review
　　(ii)　　Manpower Review
　　(iii)　　Performance Review

Organisation and Manpower Management

(iv) Management by Objectives
(v)   Training
(vi) Succession Planning
(vii) Career Planning

Manpower development activities are interrelated, as shown in Fig. 3, and, in this sense, it would be possible to talk about a 'program' of management development where the process consists of education and training, career planning and succession planning activities which are derived from the outcome of the organisation, manpower and performance reviews.

Organisation Review

Management development is closely related to organisation development, which focuses attention on people and the social system in which they work— individuals, working groups and the relationships between them — and uses various educational activities which may aim primarily to develop teamwork but also provide training for the individuals concerned. Management development appears to focus attention more on individuals than on groups and relationships, but it must do this with the context of the needs of the organisation as a whole.

Management development activities should therefore be founded upon a review of the objectives, structure and plans of the organisation (Fig. 3 below) and the implications of present weaknesses and future demands on managerial requirements.

Manpower Review

The organisation review leads naturally into a review of manpower resources. This is the manpower planning aspect of management development and, where the circumstances permit, it implies an analysis of the present resources and future requirements in terms of numbers, types and knowledge and skills. This is a general review, and individual and management succession needs would be analysed separately, although performance reviews will provide information on strengths and weaknesses that affect the overall plan.

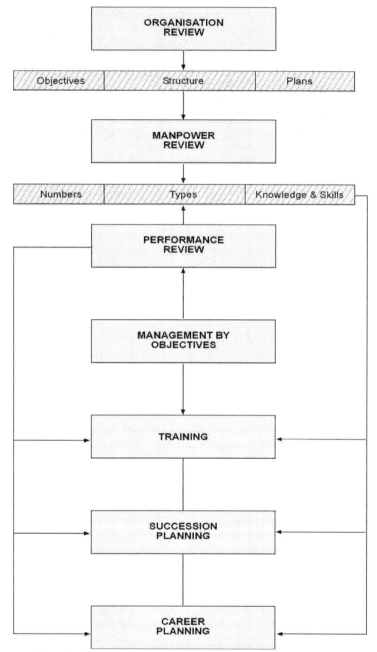

Fig. 3: The Process of Management Development

Performance Review

Performance review systems are used to identify development needs by highlighting strengths and weaknesses and, so far as this is possible, potential for promotion. They are also a basis for the counselling and coaching activities which should form the most important part of an individual's development within the company. Performance review is a systematic method of obtaining, analysing and coding information about a person that is needed:

    (a) for the better running of the business;

    (b) by the manager to help him to improve the job holder's performance and plan his career;

    (c) by the job holder to assist him to evaluate his own performance and develop himself.

There are three main groups of performance review activities:

(i) Performance Reviews which relate to the need to improve the performance of individuals and thereby to improve the effectiveness of the organisation as a whole. The purpose is to analyse what a person has done and is doing in his job in order to help him to do better, by developing his strengths or by overcoming his weaknesses.

(ii) Potential Reviews which attempt to deal with the problem of predicting the level and type of work that the individual will be capable of doing in the future. This requires the analysis of existing skills, qualities and how they can be developed to the mutual advantage of the company and the employee, as well as the identification of any weaknesses which must be overcome if the employee's full potential is to be achieved. There is also an important counselling aspect to the review of potential which consists of discussions with the individual about his aspirations and how these can best be matched to the future foreseen for him.

(iii) Reward Reviews which relate to the distribution of such rewards as pay, power and status. In any company where rewards such as salary increments or bonuses are related to performance, there has to be some method of linking the two together. In some procedures, the rate of progression through

Jacob W. Chikuhwa

a salary bracket or the size of the increment is derived from an overall assessment of performance, so that a top 'A' rating may result in a 10% merit increment while a middling 'C' rating may result in an average increment of 5%, or whatever inflationary conditions, the financial position of the company and current pay regulations allow.

Management by Objectives

Management by objectives is essentially a method of managing organisations and people and of improving the performance of managers who should, in turn, strive to improve the performance of their subordinates. This is a dynamic system which aspires to integrate the company's goals, technology and structure to achieve its profit and growth with the manager's and subordinate's need to contribute and develop themselves. The basic processes are:

(a) Subordinates agree with their managers the objectives of their job — expressed as targets or standards of performance for each key result area. The individual objectives are in line with unit and organisational objectives and are defined in a way which emphasises the contribution they make to achieving departmental and corporate plans.

(b) Performance is reviewed jointly by the manager and the subordinate to compare results with the defined objectives and standards.

(c) The manager and subordinates agree where improvements are required and how better results can be achieved and, as necessary, re-define targets and standards.

(d)   In behavioural science terms, 'An effective management must direct the vision and efforts of all managers towards a common goal. It must ensure that the individual manager understands what results are demanded of him. It must ensure that the superior understands what to expect of each of his subordinate managers. It must motivate each manager to maximum efforts in the right direction. And while encouraging high standards of workmanship, it must make them the means to the end of business performance rather than the ends in themselves.'

Organisation and Manpower Management

Management by objectives is most effective when managers recognise for themselves — with or without encouragement — that it is something they can use to their own advantage. It is even more effective if they are allowed the maximum amount of freedom to apply it in their departments in their own way — let them develop their own forms, if they want to use them. If not, let them do without. The agreed objectives can be written out on a loose piece of paper if they prefer it that way — as long as they can find the piece of paper when it comes to a review.

Training

Management development is sometimes seen as primarily a matter of providing a series of appropriate courses at various points in a manager's career. But the best definition of training is the modification of behaviour through experience, which means that managers will develop best if they receive their training in the 'real' guided self-analysis.

The principal method by which managers can be equipped is by ensuring that they have the right variety of experience, in good time, in the course of their careers. This experience can and should be supplemented, but never replaced, by courses carefully timed and designed to meet particular needs. It is necessary to state that while training is an important part of management development, it should not be allowed to degenerate into no more than a series of formal courses, even when these are based on elaborate job descriptions, job analyses and performance review systems. This guarantees a static and increasingly irrelevant approach. Formal training courses should only be used when it is essential to supplement what managers are learning on the job. It is important to understand where there may be gaps in the organisation to help identify the types of training needed.

The key management development activity is therefore ensuring that managers are given the chance to learn; and this is primarily a matter of encouraging and stimulating on the job training and providing career opportunities to broaden experience.

The training techniques may be classified into three groups according to where they are generally used:

(a) On the job techniques — demonstration, coaching, job rotation/planned experience.

Jacob W. Chikuhwa

(i) Demonstration is the technique of telling or showing a trainee how to do a job and then allowing him to get on with it. It is the most commonly used training method.

(ii) Coaching is a personal on the job training technique designed to develop individual skills, knowledge and attitudes. The term is usually reserved for management or supervisory training where informal, but planned encounters take place between managers and subordinates.

(iii)Finally, job rotation/planned experience aims to broaden experience by moving people from job to job or department to department. It can be an inefficient and frustrating method of acquiring additional knowledge and skills unless it is carefully planned and controlled. What has sometimes been referred to as the 'Cook's Tour' method of moving trainees (usually management trainees) from department to department has incurred much justified criticism because of the time wasted by trainees in departments where no one knew what to do with them or cared.

(b) On the job or off the job techniques — job (skill) instruction, question and answer assignments, projects, guided reading.

(i) Job (skill) instruction techniques should be based on skills analysis and learning theory. The sequence of instruction should follow four stages: 1) preparation, 2) presentation — explanation and demonstration and demonstration, 3) practice and testing and 4) follow-up

(ii) The question and answer technique consists of an exchange between trainer and trainees to test understanding, stimulate thought or extend learning. It may take place during a job instruction programme or as a discussion period on a formal management course.

(iii) Assignments are a specific task or investigation which an individual does at the request of his trainer or manager.

(iv) Projects are broader studies or tasks which trainees are asked to complete, often with only very generalised guidelines from their trainer or manager. They encourage initiative in seeking and analysing information, in originating ideas and in preparing and presenting the results of the project.

Organisation and Manpower Management

(v) Lastly, knowledge can be increased by giving trainees books, hand-outs or company literature and asking them to read and comment on them.

(c) Off the job techniques — lecture, talk, discussion, 'discovery' method, case study, role playing, group exercise, group dynamics (team building), business game, programmed learning.

(i) A lecture is a talk with little or no participation except a question and answer session at the end. It is used to transfer information to an audience with controlled content and timing.

(ii) A talk is a less formal lecture for a smaller group of not more than 20 people which gives plenty of time for discussion.

(iii) The objectives of using discussion techniques are 1) get the audience to participate actively in learning; 2) give people an opportunity of learning from the experience of others; 3) help people to gain understanding of other points of view; and 4) develop powers of self-expression.

(iv) The discovery method is a style of teaching that allows the trainee to learn by finding out principles and relationships for himself. The essence of the method is that the training designer thinks out the progression of problems which the trainee is required to solve, relate this progression to the capacity of the trainee, and ensures that learning is based on intrinsic factors. In other words, the trainee does not need to rely on previous knowledge and experience, nor does he depend on outside assistance (i.e. extrinsic factors).

(v) A case study is a history or description of an event or set of circumstances which is analysed by trainees in order to diagnose the causes of a problem and work out how to solve it.

(vi) In role playing, the participants act out a situation by assuming the roles of the characters involved. The situation will be one in which there is interaction between two people within a group.

(vii) In a group exercise, the trainees examine problems and develop solutions to them as a group. The problem may be a case study or it could be a problem entirely unrelated to everyday work.

(viii) Group dynamics has three interconnected and often overlapping aims: 1) to improve the effectiveness with which groups operate (team building); 2) to increase self-understanding and

Jacob W. Chikuhwa

awareness of social processes and 3) to develop interactive skills which will enable people to function more effectively in groups. Group training can also help in modifying individual attitudes and values.

(ix) A business game is an educational tool to test and develop a trainee's management skills and business knowledge. Players can see if they have what it takes to climb the corporate ladder, all the way to the top job. A trainee should correctly answer some (10 to 20) business-related multiple-choice questions in the allocated time and successfully climb some 8 levels of the corporate ladder — all the way to the top CEO job! When trainees play the game, their score is posted to the Leader Board and, thus, can discover where they are ranked on the Leader Board. Have they achieved the highest salary at CEO level?

 (x) Programmed learning consists of a text which progressively feeds information to trainees. After each piece of information, questions are posed which the trainee should answer correctly before moving on.

Succession Planning

The aim of management succession planning is to ensure that as far as possible suitable managers are available to fill vacancies created by promotion, retirement, death, leaving or transfer. It also aims to ensure that a cadre of managers is available to fill the new appointments that may be established in the future.

The information for management succession planning comes from organisation and manpower reviews and assessments of performance and potential. This information needs to be recorded so that decisions can be made on promotions and replacements, and training or additional experience arranged for those with potential or who are earmarked for promotion.

Career planning

Career planning has two aims: first, to ensure that men and women of promise are given a sequence of experience that will equip them for whatever level of responsibility they have the ability to reach; secondly, to provide individuals with potential with the guidance and encouragement they may need if they are to fulfil their potential and remain with the organisation.

Career planning is most effective when it is linked to management succession planning so that the experience and training provided is leading towards a job that has to be filled. The extent to which careers can be planned, however, is limited if it is difficult to forecast replacement needs, assess long-term potential or provide an appropriate sequence of experience. These difficulties exist in most organisations and it is usually only possible to plan the next step towards promotion. But even that is better than leaving everything to chance.

Career planning may involve counselling individuals on their possible career paths and what they must do to achieve promotion. This does not mean that a long-range plan consisting of a number of predetermined steps can be revealed. It is seldom, if ever, possible to be precise about long-term career prospects. Even if it were possible, it would be dangerous either to raise expectations which might not be fulfilled or to induce a feeling of complacency about the future. It may be feasible to talk about the next step, but beyond that, the wisest approach is to do no more than provide — in planning jargon — a scenario of the opportunities that might become available. Career counselling should not be concerned with making what might turn out to be empty promises. Its main aim should be to help the individual concerned to help himself/herself by giving him/her some idea of the direction in which he/she ought to be heading.

PART TWO

2. FINANCIAL CONTROL

2.1 Organisation/Business Objectives

Financial control is defined as keeping costs to an agreed level, ensuring that a project is developed within budget. Critically, all managers should take responsibility for financial management and should not assume that this falls within the remit of the accounts team alone. Strategic or long-term planning is also a critical building block for effective financial control. This planning can help you to decide where your financial priorities lie and how much of your total budget can be allocated to different areas of the company or project.

Whether running or setting up a business, getting a first taste of responsibility accounts or taking a business course, the first steps towards an understanding of finance are the most difficult. The consequences of failing to understand business finance are not the same for everyone. The student simply fails an exam, while the businessman all too often loses his business, and the executive gets fired.

Competition is generally greater today and the margin for mistakes smaller. Indeed, the first years of the 1980s saw the trend of business failures rising rapidly. The largest number of failures is in the early years, and the single most common cause is poor financial control. People running small businesses frequently leave financial questions to their accountants to sort out at the year end. They often have the mistaken belief that keeping the books is an activity quite divorced from the 'real' task of getting customers or making products.

By the time the first set of figures is prepared, most small businesses are already too far down the road to financial failure to be saved. The final accounts become all too final and a good business proposition has been ruined by financial illiteracy. The few businessmen who do ask the way, perhaps of an accountant or bank manager, often do not understand the terms being used to explain the situation.

An understanding of financial reports is essential to anyone who wants to control a business, but simply knowing how these reports are constructed is not enough. To be effective, the businessman must be able to analyse and interpret that financial information.

It is highly likely that a business will want to borrow money either to get started or expand. Bankers and other sources of finance will use specialised techniques to help them decide whether or not to invest. These techniques are the same as those used by the prudent businessman.

The starting point for any useful analysis is some appreciation of what should be happening in a given situation.

There are universal methods of measuring what is happening in a business. All businesses have two fundamental objectives in common which allow us to see how well (or otherwise) they are doing:

   (a) making a satisfactory return on investment and
   (b) maintaining a sound financial position.

Making a Satisfactory Return on Investment

One of the main reasons for starting a business is to make a satisfactory return on investment (profit) on the money invested. One of the well-known returns on investment is the building society deposit rate. In recent years, this has ranged between six and 12%, so for every $1,000 invested, depositors received between $60 and $120 return, each year. Their capital, in this example $1,000, remained intact and secure. To be 'satisfactory', the return must meet four criteria:

   (i)   It must give a fair return to shareholders bearing in mind the risk they are taking. If the venture is highly speculative and the profits are less than the building society interest rates, your shareholders (yourself included) will not be happy.

   (ii)   You must make enough profit to allow the company to grow. If a business wants to expand sales, it will need more working capital and eventually more space or equipment. The fastest and surest source of money for this is internally generated profits, retained in the business — reserves. *It is indicated in the Balance Sheet that a business has three sources of new money*: share capital or the owner's money;

Jacob W. Chikuhwa

loan capital, put up by banks etc.; retained profits, generated by the business.

Table 1: Profit and Loss Account for Years 1 and 2

ITEM	$	$	%	$	$	%
SALES		100 000	100,0		130 000	100,0
Cost of Sales						
Materials	30 000		30,0	43 000		33,0
Labour	20 000	50 000	20,0	25 000	68 000	19,0
Gross Profit		50 000	50,0		62 000	48,0
EXPENSES						
Rent, Rates, etc.	18 000			20 000		
Wages	12 000			13 000		
Advertising	3 000			3 000		
Total Expenses	-	33 000		2 000	38 000	
Operating or Trading Profit		17 000	17,0		24 000	18,5
Deduct Interest on:						
Overdraft	900			800		
Loan	1 250	2 150		1 250	2 050	
Net Profit before Tax		14 850	14,8		21 950	16,8
Tax Paid		5 940			8 750	
Net Profit after Tax		8 910	8,9		13 200	10,1

(iii) The return must be good enough to attract new investors or lenders. If investors can get a greater return on their money in some other comparable business, then that is where they will put it.

(iv) The return must provide enough reserves to keep the real capital intact. This means that you must recognise the impact inflation has on the business. A business retaining enough

Table 2: Balance Sheet for Year Ends 1 and 2

ITEM	$	$	$	$	$	$
FIXED ASSETS						
Furniture & Fixtures			12 500			28 110
WORKING CAPITAL						
Current Assets						
Stock	10 000			12 000		
Debtors	13 000			13 000		
Cash	100	23 100		500	25 500	
Less Current Liabilities						
Overdraft	5 000			6 000		
Creditors	1 690	6 690		5 500	11 500	
Net Current Assets			16 410			14 000
Capital Employed			28 910			42 110
FINANCED BY:						
Owner's Capital	10 000			18 910		
Profit Retained	8 910		18 910	13 200		32 110
Long-term Loan			10 000			10 000
TOTAL			28 910			42 110

profits each year to meet 5% growth in assets is actually contracting by 5% if inflation is running at 10%.

There are a number of ways in which return on capital employed (ROCE) can be measured, but for a small business, two are particularly important. The ROCE is calculated by expressing the profit before long-term loan interest and tax as a proportion of the total capital employed. Thus, if you look at Starlight Profit and Loss Account above (Table 1), you can see that for year 1, the profit before tax is $14,850. To this, we

Jacob W. Chikuhwa

have to add the loan interest of $1,250. If we did not do this, we would be double counting our cost of loan capital by expecting a return on a loan which had already paid interest. This makes the profit figure $16,100. We also ignore tax charges, not because they are unimportant or insignificant, but simply because the level of tax is largely outside the control of the business and it is the business's performance we are trying to measure.

Now look at the Balance Sheet (Table 2 above). The capital employed is the sum of the owner's capital, the profit retained and the long-term loan, in this case $28,910 ($10,000 + $8,910 + $10,000). Thus, the ROCE ratio for the first year is:

$$\frac{\$16,100}{\$28,910} = 0.56 \text{ which expressed as a percentage} = 56\%$$

The great strength of this ratio lies in the overall view it takes of the financial health of the whole business. If you look at the same ratio for the second year, you will see a small change. The ratio gives no clue as to why this has happened — it simply provides the starting point for an analysis of business performance, and an overall yardstick with which to compare absolute performance.

The second way a small business would calculate a return on capital is by looking at the profit available for shareholders — return on shareholders' capital (ROSC). This is not the money actually paid out, for example, as dividends, but is a measure of increase in 'worth' of the funds invested by shareholders.

In this case, the net profit after tax is divided by the owner's capital plus the retained profits (these although not distributed, belong to the shareholders). Thus, in our example this would be the sum:

$$\frac{\$8,910}{\$18,910} = 0.47 \text{ which expressed as a percentage} = 47\%$$

And for the second year this ratio would be 41%.

Maintaining a Sound Financial Position

As well as making a satisfactory return, investors, creditors and employees expect the business to be protected from unnecessary risks.

Clearly, all businesses are exposed to market risks: competitors, new products and price changes are all part of a healthy commercial environment. The sort of unnecessary risks that investors and lenders are particularly concerned about are high financial risks.

Cash flow problems are not the only threat to a business's financial position. Heavy borrowings can bring a high interest burden to a small business. This may be acceptable when sales and profits are good, and when times are bad, shareholders can be asked to tighten their belts. Bankers, however, expect to be paid all the time. Thus, business analysis and control are not just about profitability, but about survival and the practice of sound financial discipline.

All analysis of financial information requires comparisons. First, you can see how well you are meeting a personal goal. For example, you may want to double sales or add 25% to profits. In a more formalised business, this activity would be called budgeting, then comparisons would be made between actual results and the budget.

Second, you might want to see how well you are doing this year compared with last, or this month as opposed to the last, comparing performance against an historical standard. This is the way in which growth in sales or profits is often measured.

Thirdly, you may want to see how you are doing compared with someone else's business, perhaps a competitor, or someone in a similar line of business elsewhere. This may provide useful pointers to where improvements can be made, or to new and more profitable opportunities.

2.2 Budgeting for a Business

Everyone has made a budget or plan at some time. In our personal lives, we are always trying to match the scarce resource 'pay' with the ever expanding range of necessities and luxuries in the market place, a battle we all too often lose, with mortgage costs, or running expenses, food and children's clothes taking more cash out than we put in.

Temporary shortages of cash are made up by taking out an overdraft, the judicious use of a credit card, or talking to a rich aunt.

A business has to do much the same type of budgeting and planning, although much more thoroughly if it wants to survive and prosper. A

Jacob W. Chikuhwa

business's environment is much more complex than an individual's. For example, most people have only one source of income, and the amount of money they are likely to get in any one year is fairly easy to predict accurately. Even the smallest business has dozens or even hundreds of potential sources of income — but forecasting how much they will spend is not so easy. Some small businesses start off with their plans in the owner's head or on the back of the proverbial envelope. Most of these businesses end up going broke in the first year. There are simply not enough 'rich aunts' to go round.

The central problem is that to make a profit, a business must take risks. A small new business must take many more risks than an established or larger one, with each risk having more important consequences if things go wrong.

There is no way to eliminate all risks in business. Successful entrepreneurship is all about anticipating the sort of risks that have to be taken, and understanding how they will affect the business. This knowledge is then used as the basis of a plan or budget. Putting this information together usually means gathering facts and opinions on the market place; interpreting their probable impact on your business; deciding what you want to happen; and finally deciding how you intend to make things happen — in other words, developing your strategy.

The small business that starts its life with a well thought through plan has great advantages over the businessman who sits on 'his buttocks' as they call it in Shona — *kugarira magaro*. For a start, the plan or budget acts as a means of communicating your intentions to four vitally important audiences: the entrepreneur, the staff, shareholders and the providers of finance. You can experiment with various sales levels, profit margins and growth rates to arrive at a realistic picture of how you would like your business to develop, before committing yourself to a particular course of action.

Bankers or shareholders outside the business will be more likely to be supportive if they see that the owner/manager knows what he wants to happen, and how to make it come about. For example, they will not be surprised by calls for cash to finance sales growth, or capital expenditure if they have seen the plans in advance.

Financial Control

Most people who start up in business are fairly competitive. The budget acts as a standard against which they can measure their own business performance. This is particularly important for a new business in its first trading period, with no history to go on. In other words, you cannot really try to do better than last year, if there wasn't one. Thus, the only guide available is a realistic and achievable plan.

An attempt at planning invariably begs the question, 'How far ahead should I plan?' The answer, 'As far ahead as you can usefully see,' is not particularly helpful but it is the one most frequently given. Some guidelines that may help bring the planning horizon into view are:

(i)   Outsiders, such as bankers may have a standard period over which they expect you to plan, if you want to borrow money from them. Usually, this is at least three years, and for a new business preparing its first plan, three years is probably at the horizon itself.

(ii)   The Payback Period is another useful concept. If it is going to take you four or five years to recover your original investment and make a satisfactory profit, then that is how far you may want to plan. The payback period is a popular technique for evaluating capital investment decisions. It compares the cash cost of the initial investment with the annual net cash inflows (or savings) that are generated by the investment. This goes beyond simply calculating profit as shown in the Starlight Profit and Loss Account, which is governed by the realisation concept. The timing of the cash movements is calculated. That is, for example, when debtors will actually pay up, and when suppliers will have to be paid. By using cash in both elements, it is comparing like with like.

(iii) The Rate of Technology Change is yet another yardstick used in deciding how far ahead to plan. If your business is high-tech, or substantially influenced by changes in technology, then that factor must influence your choice of planning horizon. Companies in the early stages of the computer business which looked only three years ahead would have missed all the crucial technological trends, and as

Jacob W. Chikuhwa

technological trends are vital factors influencing the success of any business in this field, the planning time horizon must accommodate them.

The following example will illustrate the method.

Table 3: Payback Period Method

DESIGNATION	$
Initial Cost of Project	10 000
Annual Net Cash Inflows	2 000
Year 1	2 000
Year 2	4 000
Year 3	4 000
Year 4	2 000
Year 5	1 000

The payback period is three years. That is when the $10 000 initial cash cost has been matched by the annual net cash inflows of $2 000; $4 000; $4 000 of the first three years.

Every business must plan its first year in considerable detail. As well as a description of what the business is going to do, these plans should be summarised into month-by-month cash flows projection (in cash business such as a shop you may need to project cash flow on a weekly basis); a comprehensive quarterly Profit and Loss Account; and a full opening and closing position Balance Sheet. This first year plan is usually called the budget.

Future years could be planned in rather less detail, giving only quarterly cash flow projections, for example. If the planning horizon is very long, plans for the final years could be confined to statements about market (and technological) trends, anticipated market share and profit margins.

As a measure of business profitability, bankers usually look at profit margins. Any analysis of a business must consider the current level of sales activity. If you look at Starlight Profit and Loss Account (Table 1), you will see that materials consumed in sales have jumped from $30 000 to $43 000 a rise of 43%. However, a quick look at the change in sales activity will show that the situation is nothing like so dramatic. Materials, as a percentage of sales, have risen from 30% to 33% (30 000/100 000 = 30% and 43 000/130 000 = 33%). Obviously, the more you sell, the more you must make.

To understand why there have been changes in the level of return on capital employed, we have to relate both profit and capital to sales activity. The ROCE equation can be expanded to look like this:

$$\frac{\text{Profit}}{\text{Capital}} = \frac{\text{Profit}}{\text{Sales}} \times \frac{\text{Sales}}{\text{Capital}}$$

This gives us two separate strands to examine — the profit strand and the capital strand. The first of these is usually called *profit margins*.

One final point before we look at how the budget and plans are prepared. There is a tendency to think of the budgeting process as a purely financial exercise, rather theoretical and remote from the day-to-day activity of the business. This is a serious misconception, usually fostered in larger companies, where the planners and the doers lead separate existences. People who have spent time in a large organisation have to recognise that in a small business, the decision maker has to prepare his own plans. No one likes to have someone else's plans foisted upon him, a useful point to remember if a small business has a number of decision takers working in it.

In the end, an entrepreneur needs the budget and plans expressed in financial terms: cash flow forecasts, profit and loss accounts and balance sheets. But the process of preparing the budget is firmly rooted in the real business world.

2.3 An Illustrative Budget System and Related Accounting Procedures

Financial planning and control processes perform a central role in implementing the general planning activities of a business. The financial planning and control manager analyses the sales growth of the business, the investment requirements to support planned growth, and the relations

Jacob W. Chikuhwa

between revenues and costs, seeking to improve efficiency in the utilisation of funds for investment outlays and to maintain cost control as well. The budgeting processes represent a part of the broader financial

Table 4: Production Budget (Estimated 2010, First Quarter)

ITEM	Monthly Average 2009	First Month	Second Month	Third Month	Source of Data
1. Sales at $10 per unit	$10 000	$10 000	$12 000	$12 000	Assumed
2. Unit Sales	1 000	1 000	1 200	1 200	Line 1 divided by $10
3. Beginning inventory (units)	500	500	600	600	1/2 of current month's sales
4. Difference (units)	500	500	600	600	Line 2 - Line3
5. Ending inventory (units)	500	500	600	600	1/2 of current month's sales
6. Production in units	1 000	1 100	1 200	1 200	Line 4 + Line 5
7. Estimated cost of goods produced	$6 000	$6 000	$7 200	$7 200	Line 6 x $6* per unit
8. Burden absorption, under or (over)	0	(100.)	(200.)	(200.)	Line 6 x $1 000 fixed manufacturing expense
9. Adjusted cost of goods	$6 000	$6 500	$7 000	$7 000	Line 7 less Line 8
9a. Adjusted cost per unit	**$6**	$5.91	$5.83	$5.83	Line 9 divided by Line 6
10. Value of ending inventory (finished goods)	$3 000	$3 545	$3 500	$3 500	Line 5 multiplied by Line 9a (rounded)

*It has been assumed that cost of goods produced per unit = $6 and direct raw material cost $1 per unit.

planning and control systems. A complete budget system includes:

    (i) a production budget;

    (ii) a materials purchase budget;

    (iii) a budgeted, or pro forma, income statement

    (iv) a budgeted, or pro forma, balance sheet and

    (v) a capital expenditure budget.

The illustrative production budget in Table 4 above is based directly on the *sales forecast* and the estimated unit *cost of production*. It is assumed that the firm maintains its finished goods inventory at 50% of the following month's sales. In any month, the firm must produce the unit sales plus ending inventory less the beginning inventory level. The example illustrates the financial consequences of a rise in sales from $10 000-per-month level to a new plateau of $12 000. As production rises in response to increased sales, the (standard) cost of goods produced also rises. But the standard cost of goods produced increases faster than actual costs increase because of the unit cost of $6 per unit. An increase of one unit of production actually raises total costs by only $5. The estimated total cost, however, increases by $6. Estimates of the cost of goods produced are made and then adjusted by the amount of under- or over-absorbed burden. Of course, the same result for calculating the adjusted cost of goods produced (line 9 of Table 4) is obtained by multiplying $5 by the number of units produced to get total variable costs and adding $1 000 in fixed costs to reach total adjusted cost of goods produced.

The per unit adjusted costs of goods produced ($5.91) for the first month) is required to calculate the ending inventory. The first-in, first-out method of inventory costing is employed.

The level of operations indicated by the production budget is based on the sales forecast and inventory requirements. The materials purchases budget in Table 5 contains estimates of materials purchases that will be needed to carry out the production plans. Raw materials purchases depend in turn upon materials actually used in production, material costs, size of beginning inventories and requirements for ending inventory.

The example in Table 5 does not take into account economical ordering quantities (EOQs). EOQs are not integrated, primarily because

Jacob W. Chikuhwa

they assume a uniform usage rate for raw materials, an assumption that is not met in the example. Also, the EOQs analysis assumes a constant minimum inventory, but the desired minimum inventory (line 13) shifts with production levels. In a practical situation, these assumptions might be approximated. EOQs could then be used to determine optimum purchase quantities, or more sophisticated operations research techniques might be used. (See Appendix I.)

Table 5: Materials Purchases Budget

ITEM	Monthly Average 2009	First Month	Second Month	Third Month	Source of Data
11. Production in units	1 000	1 100	1 200	1 200	Line 6
12. Materials used (units)	2 000	2 200	2 400	2 400	Line 11 x 2
13. Raw materials, ending	2 200	2 400	2 400	2 400	Raw materials
Inventory					requirements next month
14. TOTAL	4 200	4 600	4 800	4 800	Line 12 + Line 13
15. Raw materials beginning Inventory	2 000	2 200	2 400	2 400	Raw materials requirements this month
16. Raw materials purchases	$2 200	$2 400	$2 400	$2 400	(Line 14 less Line 15)
					times $1

The *pro forma* accounting is a statement of the company's financial activities while excluding "unusual and nonrecurring transactions" when stating how much money the company actually made. Expenses often excluded from *pro forma* results include company restructuring costs, a decline in the value of the company's investments, or other accounting charges, such as adjusting the current balance sheet to fix faulty accounting practices in previous years.

Companies that report a *pro forma* income statement or balance sheet usually do so because the events being excluded were unusual so the GAAP (Generally Accepted Accounting Principles) financial reports required by law or accounting standards are misleading to investors and potential investors. A hypothetical crisis that happened the previous quarter is not going to recur in future quarters, so the *pro forma* results can be used by investors to forecast what a "regular" quarter might portend in the future.

The *pro forma* balance sheet, in particular, shows the projected book cash account; if all the other balance sheet accounts have transactions, *pro forma* figures and stock transactions of corporate managers. Managers must certify that they are responsible for establishing and maintaining internal controls and have designed such internal controls to ensure that material information relating to the company and its consolidated subsidiaries is made known to such managers by others within those entities, particularly during the period in which the periodic reports are being prepared.

Capital expenditure budgeting (or investment appraisal) is the planning process used to determine whether an organisation's long term investments such as new machinery, replacement machinery, new plants, new products, and research development projects are worth pursuing. It is a budget for major capital, or investment expenditures.

Cash Budget Period

Using information developed in the production and materials purchases budgets, we can generate a cash budget. In addition, estimates for other expense categories are required. In Table 6, only cash receipts from operations are considered, in order to emphasise the logic of the budget system. No account is taken of receipts or expenditures for capital items. This is because of the emphasis in this illustration on budgeting consequences of short-term fluctuations in the sales of the firm, although in practical situations it is a simple matter to incorporate capital expenditures into the Cash Budget. However, the fact that capital expenditures are ignored does not diminish their impact on cash flows.

Jacob W. Chikuhwa

Capital expenditures occur sporadically and in amounts that sometimes overwhelm operating transactions.

It is necessary to note that capital expenditures (CAPEX) are expenditures creating future benefits. A capital expenditure is incurred when a business spends money either to buy fixed assets or to add to the value of an existing fixed asset with a useful life that extends beyond the taxable year. For tax purposes, capital expenditures are costs that cannot be deducted in the year in which they are paid or incurred and must be capitalised. The general rule is that if the property acquired has a useful life longer than the taxable year, the cost must be capitalized. The capital expenditure costs are then amortized or depreciated over the life of the asset in question.

The three-month period used in the Cash Budget is not necessarily the length of the time for which a firm will predict cash flow. Although this period does coincide with the length of traditional ninety-day bank loans, a business is more likely to utilise a six-month or one-year period. Normally, a six-month forecast is prepared on a monthly basis. Briefly, the Cash Budget period will vary with the line of business, credit needs, the ability to forecast the firm's cash flows for the distant future, and requirements of funds.

Cash Budget Use

The financial manager uses the Cash Budget to anticipate fluctuations in the level of cash. Normally, a growing business will be faced with continuous cash drains. The Cash Budget tells the manager the magnitude of the outflow. If necessary, he can plan to arrange for additional funds. The Cash Budget is the primary document presented to a lender to indicate the need for funds and the feasibility of repayments.

In Table 6, the opposite situation is illustrated. The business concern will have excess cash of at least $1 000 during each of the three months under consideration. The excess can be invested, or it can be used to reduce outstanding liabilities. In this example, the business retires notes payable (Budgeted Balance Sheet, Line 49). Such a small amount as $1 000 may be held as cash or as a demand deposit, but the alert financial manager will not allow substantial amounts of cash to remain idle.

After a cash budget has been developed, two additional financial statements can be formulated: the Budgeted Income Statement (Table 7) and the Budgeted Balance Sheet (Table 9). They are prepared on an accrual rather than a cash basis. For example, the income statement accounts for depreciation charges. Expenses recognised on an accrual basis are included in total expenses (Line 32); thus, calculated net income is lowered. The only accrual item assumed in this exhibit is depreciation, and this is assumed to be $200 monthly. The before-tax profit figure in the third month in the Budgeted Income Statement (Line 33) differs from Line 26 in the Cash Budget only by the amount of depreciation. This illustration makes clear the effect of non-cash expenses on the income statement.

The Budgeted Income Statement shows the impact of future events on the business's net income. Comparison of future income with that of past periods indicates the difficulties that will be encountered in maintaining or exceeding past performance. A forecast indicating low net income should cause management to increase sales efforts as well as to make efforts to reduce costs. Anticipation and prevention of difficulties can be achieved by a sound budgeting system.

Cost of goods sold (Line 40 in Table 8) refers to the inventory costs of those goods a business has sold during a particular period. Costs are associated with particular goods using one of several formulas, including specific identification, first-in first-out (FIFO), or average cost. Costs include all costs of purchase, costs of conversion and other costs incurred in bringing the inventories to their present location and condition. Costs of goods made by the business include material, labour, and allocated overhead. The costs of those goods not yet sold are deferred as costs of inventory until the inventory is sold or written down in value.

Lenders are interested in the projected balance sheet to see what the future financial position of the business will be. Balance Sheet projections can be focused on a year-to-year forecast and assume stable underlying relations. The budget technique deals with shorter-term projections but is based on the same fundamental kind of stable relations between the volume of sales and associated asset requirements. Either method can be used, or each can operate as a check on the other. The Budgeted Balance Sheet presented in Table 9, however, is the result of a more detailed and analytical forecast of future operations. It is the

Jacob W. Chikuhwa

logical culmination of the budget system and provides a complete reconciliation between the initial Balance Sheet, the Cash Budget and the Income Statement.

The Balance Sheet looks at the bigger picture of your business comparing all your assets to all your liabilities. It tells you if you closed the business and sold everything today, how much money you would have (or how much you would owe). The reason this is called a Balance Sheet is that Assets need to balance (equal) the Liabilities. The amount you would have if everything were liquidated today is called Net Worth and is listed under Liabilities. If you have more Liabilities than Assets, the Net Worth is negative.

Table 6: Cash Budget (Estimated 2010, First Quarter)

ITEM	Monthly Average (2009)	First Month	Second Month	Third Month	Source of Data
RECEIPTS					
17. Accounts receivable					
Collected	$10 000	$10 000	$10 000	$12 000	Sales of previous month
DISBURSEMENTS					
18. Accounts payable paid	$2 000	$2 000	$2 400	$2 400	Raw materials purchases of previous month
19. Direct labour	$2 000	$2 200	$2 400	$2 400	Line 6 x $2
20. Indirect labour	$700	$700	$700	$700	Assumed
21. Variable manufacturing Expenses	1 000	1 100	1 200	1 200	Line 6 x $1
22. Insurance and taxes	100	100	100	100	Assumed
23. General and administrative	2 500	2 500	2 500	2 500	Assumed

Expenses					
24. Selling expenses	500	500	600	600	5% of Line 1
25. Total disbursements	$8 800	$9 300	$9 900	$9 900	Sum of Lines 18 through 24
26. Cash from operations	$1 200	$700	$100	$2 100	Line 17 less Line 25
26a. Initial cash	5 000	6 200	6 900	7 000	Preceding month, Line 26b
26b. Cumulative cash	6 200	6 900	7 000	9 100	Line 26 and Line 26a
27. Desired level of cash	5 000	5 000	6 000	6 000	5% of current month's Sales approx. 4.2% of annual sales
27a. Cash available (needed)					
cumulative	$1 200	$1 900	$1 000	$3 100	Line 26b less Line 27

Table 7: Budgeted Income Statement

ITEM	Monthly Average 2009	First Month	Second Month	Third Month	Source of Data
28. Sales	$10 000	$10000	$12 000	$12 000	Line 17 less Line 25
29. Adjusted cost of sales	6 000	5 955	7 045	7 000	Line 40
30. Gross income	4 000	4 045	4 955	5 000	Line 28 less Line 29
31a. General and administrative					
Expenses	2 500	2 500	2 500	2 500	Line 23
31b. Selling expenses	500	500	600	600	5% of Line 1

					Line 31a +
32. Total expenses	$3 000	$3 000	$3 100	$3 100	Line 31b
33. Net income before taxes		1 000	1 040	1 855	1 900	Line 30 less Line 32
34. Government taxes		500	522	928	950	50% of Line 33
35. Net income after taxes	$500	$523	$927	$950	Line 33 less Line 34

Table 8: Worksheet (Adjusted Cost of Sales) [Estimated 2010, First Quarter]

ITEM	Monthly Average 2009	First Month	Second Month	Third Month	Source of Data
36. Adjusted cost of goods	$6 000	$6 500	$7 000	$7 000	Line 9
37. Add: Beginning inventory		3 000	3 000	3 545	3 500	Line 10 lagged one month
38. Sum	$9 000	$9 500	$10 545	$10 500	Line 36 + Line 37
39. Less: Ending inventory		3 000	3 545	3 500	3 500	Line 10
40. Adjusted cost of goods sold*	$6 000	$5955	$7045	$7 000	Line 38 less Line 39

* Note difference from Line 9, adjusted cost of goods produced.

The required information is readily available from past balance sheets or is contained in other elements of the budget system. For example, the initial balance of notes payable is $3200. An increase in cash available (Line 27a) is used to repay notes payable, a decrease is met by additional borrowing from a commercial bank. Other new items, such as long-term debt and common stock (Lines 51 and 52), are taken from previous balance sheets.

Tables 4 to 9 present a simplified yet complete budget system that contains all the elements found in a voluminous and complex actual budget system of a business. A person who understands the logic and flow of this budget system can approach an actual budget with perspective looking for the fundamental relations involved and then applying the patterns to actual budget systems of any degree of complexity.

When formulating a capital expenditure budget, the problem to be solved is to try and determine whether ten years is long enough for the repayment of a loan of $100 000 to buy a building. As seen in our projection in Table 10, if the estimates are reliable, the working capital position of the business will be severely weakened if the loan period is held at 10 years. May be the new asset will provide profit earning capacity for fifty years, but if the business is insolvent in ten years, of the last forty years of profit may not be realised!

An important use of the statement of working-capital changes is to monitor operations in divisions that have much decision-making autonomy. That is, two divisions may be similar in earning power, which can be judged by the income statement, but one may be supporting these profits by unwise financial management — which can be judged by an analysis of working-capital changes.

An analysis of data in working capital for several past periods provides management with information on the major sources of financing used, the size and frequency of capital expenditures, the relative use of inside versus outside financing, the size of dividend payments relative to internally generated funds. The analysis of working-capital statements also helps to alert management to the possibility that one department may be borrowing money at unfavourable interest rates or under conditions of adverse maturity dates, while another department may be building up excess working capital or retiring (early) loans which have favourable interest rates.

Budget Preparation

All large companies and government units, such as schools, use budgets as an aid in management planning and control. A budget is a written plan in action in numerical form, covering a specific period of time against which actual performance may be compared. The customary coverage for an operating budget is a year, which is then broken down into quarters or months. This breakdown is particularly important for firms that have seasonal variations although the major

Jacob W. Chikuhwa

purpose is to allow for checking the budget against actual operations at frequent intervals.

Table 9: Budgeted Balance Sheet (Estimated 2010, First Quarter)

ITEM	Monthly Average 2009	First Month	Second Month	Third Month	Source of Data
ASSETS					
41. Cash	$5000	$5 000	$6 000	$6 000	Line 27
42. Government securities	-	-	-	-	-
43. Net receivables	10 000	10 000	12 000	12 000	Sales of current month
44. Inventories: Raw materials	2 200	2 400	2 400	2 400	Line 13
Finished goods	3 000	3 545	3 500	3 500	Line 10
45. Current assets	$20 200	$20 945	$23 900	$23 900	Total Lines 41 through 44
46. Net fixed assets	80 000	79 800	79 600	79 400	$80 000 less $2 000 depreciation per month
47. Total assets	$100 000	$100 745	$103 500	$103 300	Total Lines 45 and 46
LIABILITIES					
48. Accounts payable	$2 200	$2 400	$2 400	$2 400	Line 16
49. Notes payable, $3 200	2 000	1 300	2 200	100	$3 200 less Line 27a
50. Provision for Government income tax	500	1 022	1 950	2 900	Accumulation of Line 34
51. Long-term debt	25 000	25 000	25 000	25 000	Assumed
52. Common stock, $50 000	50 000	50 000	50 000	50 000	Assumed

53. Retained earnings, $20 000	20 000	21 023	21 950	22 900	Accumulation of Line 35 + $20 001
54. Total claims	$100 200	$100 745	$103 500	$103 300	Sum of Lines 48 through 53

Table 10 Projected Statement of Changes in Working Capital (10 years)

ITEM	Monthly Average 2009	Projection (10 Years)	Source of Data
SOURCES			
55. Operations	$10 000	$100 000	Line 1
56. Operations Increase possible because of acquisition of new assets	-	40 000	Assumed
57. Total from operations	10 000	140 000	Line 55 + Line 56
58. Proceeds from sale of fixed assets	-	-	-
59. Proceeds from current debt proposed	10 000	100 000	Assumed
60. Proceeds from additional outside	-	-	-
61. Total Sources	$20 000	$240 000	Total Lines 57 through 60
USES			
62. Purchase of additional fixed assets now	-	$100 000	Assumed
63. Estimated replacement of plant and equipment during 10 years		40 000	Assumed
64. Repayment of debt 10 years hence	-	100 000	Assumed
65. Regular dividend payments	-	40 000	Assumed
65a Total Uses		$280 000	
66. Estimated decrease in working capital			

			Line 65a minus
with 10-year loan	-	$40 000	Line 61

Within a company, budgets typically are prepared for: sales, sales expenses and advertising, production in all major departments, cash and estimates of the financial statements. Preparation of any budget should be completed prior to the first day of the budget period. As operations move into the budgeted period, controls should be established so that corrective measures or revisions can be made promptly.

All the activities of a business depend primarily on the volume of sales. Thus, the *first step* in the preparation of a company budget is to establish the *sales budget*. All the other departmental budgets, such as the production budget are then set up on the basis of their relation to the sales budget.

Zero-Base Budgeting

In traditional budgeting, a manager simply adds to or subtracts from a previous year's budget to arrive at a new one. In recent years a new budgeting concept called zero-base budgeting (ZBB) has been adopted by some firms. ZBB requires the budget requests to be justified in detail from scratch — or zero each year. A manager must be able to show why any money should be spent at all.

A basic advantage of ZBB is the efficiency it brings to an organization. This is because ZBB requires the gathering of detailed information that helps managers to revaluate their operations.

In ZBB, projects are ranked and priorities are assigned. As a result, some projects are either eliminated, budgeted at a reduced level, budgeted at a similar level, or increased. ZBB attacks duplication and vested interests that have escaped serious review under the traditional budgeting methods.

Budgetary Control

Budgetary control is achieved by the use of tables or forms which show the budget figures for a period of time, such as a month, with a column for inserting actual performance reports as soon as they are compiled. A comparison (variation column) between the planned and actual results indicates how well each department and the entire organisation are doing in measuring up to its budgeted figures. Any variations will be noted and corrective steps, if required, can be taken. For example, if sales in a certain territory are running below the budget, the sales manager can get in touch with the salespersons in that area to discover the cause of the trouble. All variations exceeding +10% or below -10% should be explained. This is a basic requirement, but the figure (+-10%) may vary from company to company.

Audits

In an on-going concern, the connection between audits, accounts and statistics is obvious. The main objective of an audit is to reveal loopholes in given control systems. Accounts involve the recording, classifying and summarising of business transactions, and the interpretation of this compiled information. One of the most commonly used methods for handling quantitative data is statistics. Business statistics deals with numerical (accounting) data related to the problems of business and, like accounts, involves: capturing (recording); checking; calculating and collation; presentation; and interpretation.

Thus, an audit is an independent opinion activity conducted within an organization for the review of its operations covered by its accounting system. An audit may be internal or external, depending on who is conducting it. In a Finance Department "housing" three branches, namely; accounts, internal audit and economics and statistics, an internal audit branch may act as a link between the accounts branch and the econo-stats branch. Specifically speaking, on revealing certain loopholes and/or irregularities in the accounting systems, the internal auditors should advise the econo-stats branch on the shortcomings and/or weaknesses in the accounting systems designed or forecasting methods applied for use in the financial forecasts and budget preparations by the accounts branch.

An external audit is an independent opinion activity executed by persons outside the organization. As well as being a periodic examination and evaluation of the accounting records of a business, it is conducted by a firm of certified public accountants.

When classified according to their subject matter, two common types of audits are the financial audit and the management audit. A special kind of audit — the corporate social audit — defines corporate social responsiveness.

Jacob W. Chikuhwa

Financial Audit

A financial audit is an examination and evaluation of the accounting systems and other monetary control systems of a firm. The auditors examine the accounting transactions in accordance with generally accepted auditing standards and designed media of recording of the accounts data. When deviations are found, the auditors suggest various corrective actions. Since so many measures of performance are based upon financial information, accurate financial records are necessary for effective managerial control.

Management Audit

A management audit is a detailed analysis of the overall operations of a company. It may be an internal or external audit. It is concerned with the relationships among areas of the firm. Each activity of a company is carefully examined and evaluated. Actual performance is compared with expected performance. Inefficient operations can be identified so that improvements can be made. A management audit also serves as a check on the effectiveness of the other marginal controls.

Corporate Social Audit

A corporate social audit is a systematic attempt to measure and evaluate a corporation's impact on society. This audit may be conducted by internal or external auditors and may focus of a few or many of a company's activities. Further, the company's social performance may be reported in financial or non-financial terms. In the USA a social performance index was developed by the US Chamber of Commerce. This is a voluntary measure and guide to help firms see where they can be more socially active. This involves the types of social programmes a corporation decides to support. As areas of social involvements are established either by choice or by public pressure, companies will be expected to monitor and report carefully their social performance on a formal basis. Thus, some firms and trade groups already have their own social indexes; e.g. Arco has "The Social Critique", Pennsylvania Bank and Trust Company, "The Social Scorecard".

Basic Steps in Accounting Procedures

Financial Control

Accounts and business statistics involve seven basic steps. It should be noted that the most important function of business statics is to require the manager to explain situations or to state problems in a specific form.

(i)   Data Capture: This is where figures and facts (data) are recorded on specially designed forms or source documents. Business transactions are entered in chronological order into a journal, which is a book of original entry. Although some small firms rely on pen-and-ink records, others use adding machines, cash registers, etc. Electronic data processing has made rapid strides in performing this first step as well as the other steps. Financial statements, purchase invoices, sales reports and payroll records can supply vital information that is subject to statistical analysis.

(ii)   Data Checking: This involves the following operations: verifying of data which involves checking or validating of data to ensure that they were recorded correctly; classification of data which involves placing of data elements into specific categories which provide meaning for the user. For example, journal entries are transferred to a ledger. Here, each account brings together all transactions affecting one item such as cash or sales. At stated periods (monthly, quarterly, semi-annually, or annually) the ledger accounts are totalled, or balanced. These accounts provide the basic information for financial statements; arranging (sorting) of data which involves placing data elements in a specified or predetermined sequence; controlling of data which involves control to detect missing entries and illogical or unlikely entries.

(iii)   Data Calculation: This is the step where data are input into the processing machine (an electronic calculator or a pocket calculator). Taken from the source documents or ledger, the figures are manipulated and processed. This involves: summarizing of data which involves combining or aggregating data elements into usable totals; processing of data which involves the arithmetic/logic manipulation of data to produce financial statements. Since these statements are the result of and the reason for much of the work done by an accounts branch, they are regarded essential management reports.

Jacob W. Chikuhwa

Various types of statistical measurements can be applied to produce results ready for presentation and interpretation. Two types of statistical measurement which are commonly used are ratios and percentages. Other common types of statistical measurement include averages, index numbers, correlations and time series. (See Appendix I)

(iv)   Data Collation: After the essential management reports are processed, collation is carried out by way of reference to data already in files. This involves: controlling of data to check reasonableness and accuracy. Here data are compared with previous data of a similar nature; assembling of data in order to place the calculated data elements into a format that can be understood by the user. Such statements include the profit and loss statement, balance sheet, working capital statement, etc.

(v)   Data Production: This is where the end product is produced (output). The manipulation and collation of the figures are complete and a statistical analysis is produced and stored or disseminated. The operations involved at this final stage are analysis of data to reveal the full informational content of data, the underlying relationships they contain must be identified; storage of data which implies placing of data/information into some storage media such as paper, magnetic tape, magnetic disk or microfilm or USB, where it can be retrieved when needed; retrieval of data which involves the searching out and gaining access to specific data/information elements from the medium where it is stored; and reproduction of data which involves duplicating data/information from one medium to another or into another position in the same medium.

(vi)   Data Interpretation: This step in business statistics aids management to make decisions and to control operations. However, caution should be used in relying heavily on statistical measurements to influence decision making. Despite the best of intentions, several types of errors can creep into a computation. Arithmetic errors are likely to occur, particularly when the quality of data to be processed is extensive.

(vii)   Data Presentation: This involves showing of results in a form that is easily understood. To present statistical material in a manner that will be useful for purposes of analysis, two devices are commonly used. These are summary tables and graphic presentations. The graphic presentation of statistical data has the great advantage of presenting a visual analysis of the facts. Examples of graphic statistical presentations are the line or curve chart, the bar chart, the pie diagram or circular chart.

The objectives in this final step in accounting procedures should be three fold, namely:

(a) to convey an entirely unexpected input to management;

(b) to reduce uncertainty about a future state of event. The interpretation should bring new understanding about a future state of event. The interpretation should bring new understanding by modifying the original perception; and/or

(c) to increase the knowledge level of the recipient. The fact that a business may or may not have been operated at a profit is of vital concern, but this one figure fails to tell the whole story. For example, a bank may be willing to extend a loan to a firm that has a strong financial structure despite recent operating losses. Judicious use of such borrowed funds might correct conditions so that future business operations would be profitable. On the other hand, a firm may be headed for financial trouble even though it is currently operating profitably. Therefore, one has to take a candid approach when interpreting accounting/statistical data.

2.4 Financial (Flow) Statements

(i) Cash Budget (Cash Flow Analysis): The cash budget is used as a measure to anticipate fluctuations in the level of cash. It tells management the *magnitude of cash outflows*. In addition, it indicates the combined effects of the budgeted operations on the firm's cash flows. It also helps management in making short-term credit decisions. It is the primary document presented to a lender to indicate the need for funds and the feasibility of repayment.

The cash budget shows receipts, i.e. accounts receivable collected and disbursements, i.e. accounts payable paid, purchases, wages and salaries, rent, insurance and taxes, etc. (See Table 6.)

Jacob W. Chikuhwa

(ii) Income Statement: Other names given to this statement are Profit and Loss Statement, Operating Statement, Income Summary and Income Account. The income statement is dynamic; it summarises the incomes and expenses of a business for a stated period of time such as a year, six months, a quarter or a month. It explains the *changes in net assets* which arise from operations. This can be used by management as one indication or index of the "success" of a firm. It is used to provide a basis for predicting dividend and growth potential.

The income statement show Sales, on one hand, and various Costs (general and administrative expenses, selling expenses and taxes) on the other. (See tables 1 and 7.) It is to be noted that expenses recognized on an accrual basis are included, i.e. such expenses like depreciation[1] which lowers the calculated net income. The income statement is based on a flow concept, showing what occurred between two points in time.

(iii) Balance Sheet: The balance sheet is a picture of the business at a given instant of time. It lists a firm's assets, liabilities and capital as of the close of business on a specific date – usually the end of a month, a quarter or a year. It is as a document for forward-planning intended to produce a financial position which is an improvement on the position when the planning begins. The *profit made* by a firm will be reflected in the balance sheet. The balance sheet, especially that part which represents the shareholders' interests in the firm, reflects the success or failure of the planning and control and in this sense is the final measure of efficient management.

The balance sheet shows the value of a firm's assets and of the claims on those assets at a particular point in time. The top group of assets — cash on hand and in banks, accounts owed (receivable) by its customers, inventories on hand, marketable securities, which are expected to be

---

[1] For capital budgeting purposes depreciation should be assessed against capital funds and this is the weighted cost of capital before outside equity is used. The firm could, if it so desired, distribute depreciation generated funds to its creditors and stockholders.

converted into cash within one year — is defined as current assets. Assets in the lower part of the statement — plant and equipment, buildings and land owned, which are not expected to be converted to cash within one year — are defined as fixed assets.

The right side of the balance sheet is arranged similarly. Those items towards the top of the claims column will mature and have to be paid off fairly soon; those further down the column will be due in the more distant future. Current liabilities have to be paid within one year; because the firm never has to pay off common stockholders, common stock and retained earnings represent permanent capital. The liabilities of a firm consist of the claims of its creditors against its assets. (For items in the balance sheet see Tables 2 and 9.)

Since all assets of a business are subject to claims by its creditors and owners, total assets should equal the total claims of creditors and owners. The statement that assets equal liabilities plus capital is known as the balance sheet equation and is expressed as follows:

$$\text{Assets} = \text{Liabilities} + \text{Capital}$$
$$\text{or}$$
$$\text{Assets} - \text{Liabilities} = \text{Capital}$$

The balance sheet equation stresses that a business has an entity of its own showing the amount of its obligation to its owner or owners.

(iv) Statement of Changes in Financial Position: The statement of changes in financial position shows the *sources that provided working capital*, what this working capital was used for and the components of the resulting increase or decrease in working capital. Working capital is the dollar difference between the total current assets and the total current liabilities.

The customary major source of working capital is the net income of the business. Another source of working capital, depreciation, reduces net income but does not require an outlay of cash during the current year. Other sources include the sale of securities and unneeded assets. Working capital is commonly used to pay dividends, retire long-term debt and acquire additions to property, plant and equipment.

The analysis of changes in the firm's financial position, also called statement of sources and uses of funds analysis, performs an important

Jacob W. Chikuhwa

role. If a firm requests a loan, the bank's loan officer will doubtless pose three questions: What has the firm done with the money it had? What will it do with the new funds? How will it repay the loan? The statement of changes in financial position, or sources and uses statement, helps provide answers to these questions and to others that interested parties and the firm's own management may have about the organization.

The sources of funds reflect *decreases* in working capital: reduction in cash, sale of marketable securities and increase in other liabilities. The uses of funds, on the other hand, show *increases* in working capital: inventory investment, increase in receivables, reduction in notes payable and reduction in accounts payable.

Given the projected balance sheet and supplementary projected data on earnings, dividends, and depreciation, the financial manager can construct a pro forma sources and uses of funds statement to summarise the firm's projected operations over the planning horizon. The nature of the statement typically involved is conveyed by Table 11.

The main sources of funds were net income and depreciation. The main uses of funds were additions to properties, plant and equipment. The excess of the sources of funds is related to the increase in working capital. One way to look at this is to recognize that the investment in current assets (a use of funds) exceeded the net increase in current liabilities (a source of funds) by the $96 803 000, which just balanced the excess of sources over uses of funds from other sources of $96 803 000. Thus, in practice the sources and uses of funds are divided between those that do not affect current assets and current liabilities and those that do. However, for ease of presentation it may be necessary to make this distinction in the procedures. But the format is perfectly general so that it can be modified as desired.

(v) Working Capital Statement: As stated above, the working capital statement is a reflection of current assets minus current liabilities. It is a statement expressing a firm's *investments in short-term assets*. This helps to reflect a financial history of the firm for several past periods. The statement should show the major sources of financing used, the size and frequency of capital expenditure, etc. This also helps to alert management to the possibility that one department is borrowing money at unfavourable interest rates or under conditions

Financial Control

Table 11 Consolidated Statement of Changes in Financial Position for Year Ended December 31, 2009

ITEM	2009 ($)
SOURCES OF FUNDS	
Net income	1 105 881 000
Depreciation, depletion and amortisation	621 533 000
Deferred income taxes	79 353 000
Undistributed income of unconsolidated companies	-37 073 000
Funds provided by operations	1 769 694 000
Increases in long-term debt	27 724 000
Net book value of properties, plant and equipment sold or retired	59 360 000
TOTAL SOURCES OF FUNDS	**1 856 778 000**
USES OF FUNDS	
Additional to properties, plant and equipment	1 049 673 000
Cash dividends	434 581 000
Reductions in long-term debt	264 458 000
Other net increase in investments and advances	7 589 000
Other — net	3 674 000
TOTAL USES OF FUNDS	**1 759 975 000**
Increase in Working Capital	96 803 000
Analysis of Changes in Working Capital	
Increase (Decrease) in Current Assets	
Cash and marketable securities	535 639 000
Receivables	614 143 000
Inventories	-221 310 000

	928 472 000
Decrease (Increase) in Current Liabilities	
Accounts payable	-402 180 000
Notes and loans payable	7 000 000
Current maturities of long-term debt	-208 239 000
Government and other taxes on income	-207 098 000
Other	-21 152 000
	-831 669 000
Increase in Working Capital	96 803 000

of adverse maturity dates, while another department is building up excess working capital or retiring (early) loans which have favourable interest rates.

Working capital policy is concerned with two sets of relationships among balance sheet items. The first policy question concerns the relationships among types of assets and the way these are financed. One policy for matching assets and liability maturities and financing current assets with short-term debt and fixed assets with long-term debt or equity; but this policy is unsounded because current assets represent levels of investments that increase as sales grow. If the policy is followed, the maturity structure of the debt is determined by the level of fixed versus current assets. Since short-term debt is frequently less expensive than long-term debt, the expected rate of return may be higher if more short-term debt is used. However, large amounts of short-term credit increase the risks of having to renew this debt at times of higher interest rates and of being unable to renew the debt at all if the firm experiences difficulties.

The second policy question deals with the determination of the level of total current assets to be held. Current assets vary with sales, but the ratio of current assets to sales is a policy matter. A firm that elects to operate aggressively will hold relatively small stocks of current assets, a policy that will reduce the required level of investment and increase the expected rate of return on investment. However, an aggressive policy also increases the likelihood of running out of inventories or losing sales because of an excessively tough credit policy. Both aspects of working capital policy involve risk-return trade-offs.

A projection of changes in working capital (see Table 10) will aid in determining a reasonable loan life in terms of ability to repay. For example, suppose that $500 000 is needed to buy a building in order to maintain and somewhat increase the present earning power of the firm. Is ten years long enough a repayment period? A projection of working capital from operations compared with projected divided payments, other fixed-asset purchases and other debt retirement for the next ten years will help determine whether the loan period is the proper length. The income statement will not suffice in this regard because income will explain (or project) the changes in net assets only. What is needed is a projection of the working-capital balance ten years from now.

Costing for Business Start-up

Paradoxically, one of the main reasons small businesses fail in the early stages is that too much start-up capital is used to buy fixed assets. While clearly some equipment is essential at the start, other purchases could be postponed. This may mean that 'desirable' and labour saving devices have to be borrowed or hired for a specific period. Obviously, not as nice as having them to hand all the time but if, for example, photocopiers, electronic typewriters, word processors, micros and even delivery vans are bought into business, they become part of the fixed costs. The higher the fixed cost plateau, the longer it usually takes to reach break-even and then profitability. And time is not usually on the side of the small new business. It has to become profitable relatively quickly or it will simply run out of money and die.

The process of calculating the costs of starting a small business begins with a list of all necessary purchases including tangible assets (for example, equipment, inventory) and services (for example, remodelling, insurance), working capital, sources and collateral. The budget should contain a narrative explaining how you decided on the amount of this reserve and a description of the expected financial results of business activities. The assets should be valued with each and every cost. All other expenses like labour factory overhead, all freshmen expenses are also included into business budgeting.

Jacob W. Chikuhwa

Bear in mind that different small businesses will have different types of start-up costs. For example, a furniture retailer might need a storefront and staff to man it, while a toy manufacturer might need manufacturing equipment, a warehouse and staff that is trained to operate the equipment. And then again, if you are operating an on-line retail business, you might be doing it at home, and do not need a facility or staff at all.

Costs for a business start-up can be divided up into six major categories:

(i)   Cost of Sales: Product inventory, raw materials, manufacturing equipment, shipping, packaging, shipping insurance, warehousing;

(ii)   Professional Fees: Setting up a legal structure for your business (e.g. Limited Liability Company, corporation), trademarks, copyrights, patents, drafting partnership and non-disclosure agreements, attorney fees for on-going consultation, retaining an accountant;

(iii)   Technology Costs: Capital equipment (e.g. machinery/plant, computer hardware, computer software, printers, security measures, IT consulting);

(iv)   Administrative Costs: Various types of business insurance, office supplies, licenses and permits, express shipping and postage, product packaging, parking, rent, utilities, phones, copier, fax machine, desks, chairs, filing cabinets – anything else you need to have on a daily basis to operate a business;

(v)   Sales and marketing costs: Printing of stationery, marketing materials, advertising, public relations, event or trade show attendance or sponsorship, trade association or chamber of commerce membership fees, travel and entertainment for client meetings, mailing or lead lists;

(vi)   Wages and Benefits: Employee salaries, payroll taxes, benefits, workers compensation.

Factor in the time to get your business start-up off the ground

One critical component of getting an accurate start-up cost estimate is to determine the length of time it is going to take you to open your start-up business. It might be very different if you are opening a restaurant versus an driving school. No matter what your business type, take into account everything you will spend, from the moment you dig into the start-up process, through the time you are ready to sell a product or service. If you need three months from the time you sign a lease to the time you can put the "open" sign on your retail storefront, calculate how much money you will need for salaries, electricity, rent (and your mortgage payment!) during those three months.

Learn about the specific costs for your type of new business

There is a variety of resources one can tap into to understand specific costs associated with one's chosen dream start-up business. Start with the small- to medium-sized enterprises (SMEs), where you can search for other people in your industry, and post a message on the boards asking for help from fellow entrepreneurs.

Also make sure you check out your industry's trade association

It should have an active group of members who are going through or have successfully navigated the start-up process, and they typically will be happy to share tips with you. You might even get access to sample business plans and checklists for your market niche, but most importantly, you will find out which hidden costs to be wary of in your industry.

Take every opportunity you can to network with business owners in your industry, whether it is on-line or in person. They will have the best understanding of how the costs of a typical business in your industry balance out across those six categories. With that knowledge, you will be able to create a reasonable cost estimate for starting a business of your own.

Above all, be realistic when calculating start-up costs for your new business. The first calculation may not be the right one. Continue to refine your analysis until you are satisfied with the final number, and then do yourself the favour of adding a miscellaneous line item for 10 percent of your total budget. You will spend more than you think to get your dream start-up business going, and the "miscellaneous" category will cover any unexpected costs.

Now, let us look at two hypothetical new small businesses A & B. They are both making and selling identical products at the same price, $10.

Jacob W. Chikuhwa

Table 12 Costing for Business Start-up

Company A

ITEM	DATA ($)
Unit variable cost	2,5
Fixed costs	40 000
Variable costs	25 000
Total costs	65 000
Selling price	10,0
Break-even point	40 000/(10-2,5) = 5333 units
Profit at Maximum Volume (Sales Revenue - Total Costs)	35 000

Company B

ITEM	DATA ($)
Unit variable cost	4,5
Fixed costs	20 000
Variable costs	45 000
Total costs	65 000
Selling price	10,0
Break-even point	20 000/(10-4,5) = 3636 units
Profit at Maximum Volume	35 000

They plan to sell 10 000 units each in the first year. The owner of Company A plans to get fully equipped at the start. His fixed costs will be $40 000, double that of Company B. This is largely because, as well as his own car, he has bought such things as a delivery van, new equipment and a photocopier. Much of this will not be fully used for some time, but will save some money now. This extra expenditure will result in a lower unit variable cost than Company B can achieve a typical capital intensive result. Company B's owner, on the other hand, proposes to start up on a shoestring. Only $20 000 will go into fixed costs, but of course, his unit variable cost will be higher, at $4.50. The variable cost is higher because, for example, he has to pay an outside carrier to deliver, while Company A uses his own van and pays only for petrol.

From the data on each company, you can see that total costs for 10 000 units are the same, so total possible profits, if 10 000 units are sold are also the same. The key difference is that Company B starts making profits after 3 636 units have been sold. Company A has to wait until 5 333 units have been sold.

Another pair of reasons why small businesses fail very early on is connected with the market place. They are frequently over-optimistic on how much they can sell. They also under-estimate how long it takes for sales to build up. Thus, for these reasons, and spending too much start-up capital on fixed assets, great care should be taken to keep start-up fixed costs to the minimum.

There are all sorts of 'persuasive' arguments to go for a capital intensive cost structure. In periods of high growth, the greater margin on sales will produce a higher ROCE, but high fixed costs will always expose a new or small business to higher risks. A small business has enough risks to face, with a survival rate of less than 20 percent in its first few years, without adding them.

2.5 Book-keeping

Book-keeping is the recording of financial transactions. Transactions include sales, purchases, income, and payments by an individual or organisation. Book-keeping is usually performed by a book-keeper. Book-keeping should not be confused with accounting. The accounting process is usually performed by an accountant. The accountant creates reports from the recorded financial transactions recorded by the book-keeper and files forms with government agencies.

A book-keeper (or bookkeeper), also known as an accounting clerk or accounting technician, is a person who records the day-to-day financial

Jacob W. Chikuhwa

transactions of an organisation. A book-keeper is usually responsible for writing the "daybooks". These daybooks consist of purchases, sales, receipts, and payments. The bookkeeper is responsible for ensuring all transactions are recorded in the correct daybook, suppliers' ledger, customer ledger and general ledger. The bookkeeper brings the books to the trial balance stage. An accountant may prepare the income statement and balance sheet using the trial balance and ledgers prepared by the bookkeeper

It is hard to believe that any businessman could hope to survive without knowing how much cash he has and what his profit or loss on sales is. He needs these facts on at least a monthly, weekly, or occasionally even a daily basis, to survive yet alone to grow. All too often, a new business's first set of accounts are also its last, with the firm's accountants, bank manager or creditors signalling bankruptcy. While bad luck plays a part in some failures, a lack of reliable financial information plays a part in most.

But it is not only the owner who needs those financial data. Bankers, shareholders, Collector of Taxes, etc., will be unsympathetic audiences to the businessman without well-documented facts to back him up. A bank manager faced with a request for an increased overdraft facility to help a small business grow, needs financial facts to work with. Without them he will generally have to say no, as he is responsible for other people's money.

In simple terms, the main reasons for book-keeping are:

(i)   to keep records of income (money coming in) and expenditure (money spent) so that the profit or loss during a period of time can be easily worked out;

(ii)   to keep records of assets (property and stock owned) and liabilities (bills or money still owing to others) so that the financial situation of the project or business can be worked out at any time.

Book-keeping Principles

The way a business records and stores financial facts is by keeping books. In other words, it is the process of keeping track of your business' financial transactions. The owner/manager may keep these himself at the start, if the business is small and the trading methods simple. Later on, he may feel his time could be more usefully spent helping the business to expand. At that stage, he may have a book-keeper in for a few hours, or days, a week. Or perhaps he could use an outside book-keeping service, sending the information to them periodically.

Many small retailers now have cash tills that are programmed to analyse sales, produce product gross margin information, stock levels, and even signed when and how much new stock is needed. Finally, if the work and profits warrant it, a book-keeper (or even an accountant) may be employed full time.

By staying current with book-keeping enables you to have up-to-date information about whether you are spending too much on certain types of expenses and you can take steps to remedy the situation. In addition, timely and accurate book-keeping helps the entrepreneur to pay expenses and taxes on time, which enables one to avoid penalties and late fees.

Income

Bookkeeping records should include an accurate tally of business income, including all sales and transactions that result in a payment either immediately or at some point in the future. Set up your book-keeping system to enter sales amounts at intervals that correspond to your sales rhythm. If your business relies on a limited number of large sales, track each sale individually. If your business makes numerous small sales, tally the results by day. If you receive income from multiple sources, such as several sales locations, break down your sales to track the amount transacted at each location. Tally your gross income periodically, and at least once a month.

Expenses

Set up your bookkeeping system to track your business expenses. Break down these expenses into categories such as materials, rent, labour and advertising. Tally your monthly totals in each category, and track the percentage of your gross income that you spend in each category.

Accounts Receivable

If your business makes transactions for which it does not receive immediate payment, set up your bookkeeping system to track the

Jacob W. Chikuhwa

payments that you receive on customer accounts. Develop a schedule that integrates the payment terms for each client, such as 14 or 30 days, with their purchasing history so that you know when their payments are due. Follow up with delinquent accounts by calling their bookkeeping departments and reminding them that payment is due.

Accounts Payable

Keep track of expenses that your business incurs that you pay over time, such as invoices for materials that allow payment terms such as 14 or 30 days, or utility bills with specific due dates. Stay abreast of payment schedules and plan ahead to budget for upcoming payments.

Taxes

Your business accrues taxes with virtually every transaction it makes, but pays taxes much more infrequently, such as monthly or quarterly. Keep track of taxes that you collect in the form of sales tax, and taxes that you withhold from employees' pay checks. If possible, deposit these amounts in a separate bank account and, at the very least, know how much you owe for each tax period so you do not mistake these funds for available capital. Fill out your tax forms and pay your taxes on time.

The Records to be Kept

It is essential to remember that having lots of cash, either in the till or the bank, does not mean that you are making profit. Conversely, pursuing profitable business can often lead to cash flow problems. The records must keep track of all items that affect both cash and profits.

The emergence of computerised systems has created the possibility of on-line book-keeping. Online book-keeping, or remote bookkeeping, allows source documents and data to reside in web-based applications which allow remote access for book-keepers and accountants. All entries made into the on-line software are recorded and stored in a remote location. The on-line software can be accessed from any location in the world and permit the book-keeper or data entry person to work from any location with a suitable data communications link.

There are two main methods for keeping the accounts of small businesses. These are single-entry book-keeping and double-entry book-keeping. Their names really explain themselves. The primary book-keeping record in *single-entry bookkeeping* is the cash book, which is similar to a checking (cheque) account register but allocates the income and expenses to various income and expense accounts. Separate account records are maintained for petty cash, accounts payable and receivable, and other relevant transactions such as inventory and travel expenses. These days, single-entry book-keeping can be done with DIY bookkeeping software to speed up manual calculations.

When one becomes more comfortable with bookkeeping entries, one could simplify the above entry slightly by "netting" the change in accounts receivable for the day.

In *double-entry book-keeping*, for every entry recorded, it is in fact recorded twice, whereas in single entry book-keeping, it is just recorded once. The double-entry book-keeping method is advantageous in that when mistakes and/or distortions happen (and they always do) they are much easier to find. This method can also deal with unpaid bills and accounts.

Table 13: Double-entry Book-keeping

Transaction	Debit	Credit
Cash	1 640	
Accounts receivable	450	
Sales		1 700
Accounts receivable		315
Sales tax payable		75

Transaction	Debit	Credit
Cash	1 640	
Accounts receivable	135	
Sales		1 700
Sales tax payable		75

This is a method of keeping accounting records that recognises the dual nature (source and disposition) of every financial transaction expressed by the basic accounting equation (Assets = Liabilities + Owners' Equity). In this method, every transaction is entered twice in the account books, first, to record a change in the assets' side (called a

Jacob W. Chikuhwa

'debit') and, second, to mirror that change in the equities' side (called a 'credit').

If all entries are recorded accurately, the account books will 'balance' because the total of debit entries will equal the total of credit entries. Double-entry book-keeping is used universally, except in very small or cash-transactions based firms which use 'single-entry book-keeping'.

Double-entry is used only in nominal ledgers. It is not used in daybooks, which normally do not form part of the nominal ledger system. The information from the daybooks will be used in the nominal ledger and it is the nominal ledgers that will ensure the integrity of the resulting financial information created from the daybooks (provided that the information recorded in the daybooks is correct).

In order to take control of financial recordkeeping, a businessperson must accurately record day-to-day sales, purchases, and other transactions. A daybook is a descriptive and chronological (diary-like) record of day-to-day financial transactions also called a *book of original entry*. The daybook's details must be entered formally into journals to enable posting to ledgers. Daybooks include:

(i)   Sales and revenue daybook, for recording all the sales and revenue invoices;

(ii)   Sales credits daybook, for recording all the sales credit notes;

(iii)   Purchases daybook, for recording all the purchase invoices;

(iv)   Purchases credits daybook, for recording all the purchase credit notes;

(v)   Cash daybook, usually known as the cash book, for recording all money received as well as money paid out. It may be split into two daybooks: receipts daybook for money received in, and payments daybook for money paid out.

And then there is a journal which is a formal and chronological record of financial transactions before their values are accounted for in the general ledger as debits and credits. A company can maintain one journal for all transactions, or keep several journals based on similar activity (i.e. sales, cash receipts, revenue, etc.) making transactions easier to summarize and reference later. For every debit journal entry recorded, there must be an equivalent credit journal entry to maintain a balanced accounting equation.

Financial Control

There are many software solutions on the market to help with the automation of accounting procedures. Accounting software is sold in office supply stores, software outlets, electronics stores, mail order houses, and directly from software publishers. It is advisable to look for accounting software that permits the use of passwords to control access to all or some of the business's accounting transactions.

Let us now look at some typical daily business transactions, starting with *Sales Invoices*: If you use sales invoices, you will post the information from each invoice to an entry in the sales journal. If you maintain customer charge accounts, you will also be posting entries to the accounts receivable ledgers so that each customer account is up-to-date. Sales invoices should be numbered. At a minimum, prepare two copies; give one copy to the customer, and retain the other. Preferably, you should prepare the invoices in triplicate, with two copies retained by you. File one by customer name; the other by invoice number. Include cancelled or voided invoices when filing by number, so that you can account for all of them. The invoice should show the date of the sale, quantity, if applicable, price or rate, an extension column, if applicable (quantity multiplied by price), and a payment due date.

If you use a computer software program to perform your accounting, it probably has a pre-designed sales invoice that you can use. Most office suites (such as Microsoft Office or OpenOffice.org) also contain a template that may be used as a starting point to design your own sales invoice. In addition, free templates may be found on a number of websites.

Cash Register Totals: If you use a cash register, daily sales can be totalled on the register. Most new cash registers should be able to separately record cash sales and charge sales, and keep track of sales tax. Some should also be able to record cash received on account. At the end of the business day, record your cash register totals in the sales journal.

Cash Sheets: If you do not use a cash register, you can record cash receipts on a daily cash sheet and record sales on a columnar sales register. A cash sheet is a daily reconciliation of cash received and cash paid out. If a lot of your business is transacted in cash, such as in a retail store, you should prepare a cash sheet at the end of each day. Deposit all cash receipts in your bank account daily. Your daily cash receipts should

Jacob W. Chikuhwa

generally be the same amount as your daily bank deposit. If they are not the same, you should investigate and reconcile the two amounts. Any reasons for a difference should be apparent on your cash sheet, such as a small amount of cash paid out for a miscellaneous expense.

An important reason to do a cash sheet is to alert you to any shortage or surplus of cash for the day. Some businesses that do not prepare a cash sheet simply count the cash in the register at the end of the day. Without doing reconciliation, they do not discover any shortages or overcharges. A shortage could be the result of theft, or it could simply result from your failure to record a special transaction, such as an expense you paid in cash.

Sales Registers: The sales register is simply a record of each sale for the day. Total the cash sheet and sales register at the end of the day. Enter the totals in the sales and cash receipts journal. There are many different types of sales journals and cash receipts journals available. To simplify your bookkeeping, a combined sales and cash receipts journal is recommended. If you are going to be recording sales and cash receipts manually in a journal, visit an office supply store. They will have many different kinds for you to choose from.

If you will be using computer software, you probably won't have to decide which type of journal to use. Your program will probably have some type of sales and cash receipts journal, but may allow you to customise it based on your type of business.

Petty Cash: If your customers normally pay by check, you may need to have a petty cash box so that you will have some currency on hand to pay miscellaneous small expenses. A petty cash box is not necessary if you use a cash register and always have currency on hand, as long as you keep track of these small purchases.

There is a need to have a Petty Cash Book to record transactions in notes and coins. Money in is on the left-hand page and money out on the right. The money out could include such items as stamps or office coffee etc. Always keep receipts as one day you may have to verify these records. Once a week, or daily if the sums involved justify it, total the money in and out to get cash balance. Check that it agrees with actual cash from the till or cash box.

The petty cash drawer or box should be locked when not in use. Only one person should have access to the petty cash, so that one person is held accountable for it.

Bank Reconciliation: Prepare bank reconciliation when you receive your bank statement every month. This is a very important part of your cash control procedures. It verifies the amount of cash you have in your checking account. It will also help you find bookkeeping errors and could help prevent irregularities such as employee theft.

The cash balance in your books will never agree with the balance shown on the bank statement because of the delay in checks and deposits clearing the bank, automatic bank charges and credits you have not recorded, and errors you may have made in your books. After preparing the bank reconciliation, you can be comfortable that the account balance shown on your books is up-to-date.

Another important reason to do bank reconciliation is that it may uncover irregularities such as employee theft of funds.

Here are step-by-step instructions for preparing bank reconciliation.

(i)   Prepare a list of deposits in transit: Compare the deposits listed on your bank statement with the bank deposits shown in your cash receipts journal. On your bank reconciliation, list any deposits that have not yet cleared the bank statement. Also, take a look at the bank reconciliation you prepared last month. Did all of last month's deposits in transit clear on this month's bank statement? If not, you should find out what happened to them.

(ii)   Prepare a list of outstanding checks: In your cash disbursements journal, mark each check that cleared the bank statement this month. On your bank reconciliation, list all the checks from the cash disbursements journal that did not clear. Also, take a look at the bank reconciliation you prepared last month. Are there any checks that were outstanding last month that still have not cleared the bank? If so, be sure they are on your list of outstanding checks this month. If a check is several months old and still has not cleared the bank, you may want to investigate further.

(iii)   Record any bank charges or credits: Take a close look at your bank statement. Are there any special charges made by the bank

Jacob W. Chikuhwa

that you have not recorded in your books? If so, record them now just as you would have if you had written a check for that amount. By the same token, if there are any credits made to your account by the bank, those should be recorded as well. Post the entries to your general ledger.

(iv)   Compute the cash balance per your books: Foot the general ledger cash account to arrive at your ending cash balance.

(v)   Enter bank balance on the reconciliation: At the top of the bank reconciliation, enter the ending balance from the bank statement.

(vi)   Total the deposits in transit: Add up the deposits in transit, and enter the total on the reconciliation. Add the total deposits in transit to the bank balance to arrive at a subtotal.

(vii)   Total the outstanding checks: Add up the outstanding checks, and enter the total on the reconciliation.

(viii)   Compute book balance per the reconciliation: Subtract the total outstanding checks from the subtotal in step (vi) above. The result should equal the balance shown in your general ledger.

If your bank reconciliation does not balance, you need to find the error or errors. We will look at the most conspicuous errors. Otherwise, look at the seven basic steps in accounts and business statistics on page 60/1.

(i)   Failed to record all items clearing the bank statement: Look at your bank statement carefully. Are there any items, such as miscellaneous bank charges or automatic deposits or withdrawals that were not recorded in your books?

(ii)   Failed to record a check or deposit: Did you record all checks and deposits in your journals? This should have been apparent when you were preparing your lists of deposits in transit and outstanding checks.

(iii)   Incorrectly recorded an amount: Compare each item on the bank statement with your journal entry for that item. Did you enter the correct amount?

Cash Disbursements and Purchase Journals: A cash disbursements journal is where you record your cash (or check) paid-out transactions. It can also be called a purchases journal or an expense journal.

There are many different types and styles of cash disbursements journals. If you will be recording expenses manually in a journal, visit an office supply store. They should have different types to choose from. Look at the column headings, and choose the journal that best meets the needs of your business. You might consider a disbursements journal that is integrated with your check book — this may save you some time because your journal entry is made at the same time as you write the check.

If you are using computer software, you probably won't have to decide which type of journal to use. Your program will probably have some type of disbursement and purchase journals, but may allow you to customise it based on your business needs.

Accounts Receivable: Accounts receivable are unpaid customer invoices, and any other money owed to you by your customers. The sum of all your customer accounts receivable is listed as a current asset on your balance sheet.

You should keep an accounts receivable ledger account for each customer. The accounts receivable ledger, which can also double as a customer statement, is a record of each customer's charges and payments.

When a customer purchases something, you will first record the sale in the sales and cash receipts journal. This journal will have accounts receivable debit and credit columns. Charge sales and payments on account are entered in these two columns, respectively.

Then, each day, the credit sales recorded in the sales and cash receipts journal is posted to the appropriate customer's accounts in the accounts receivable ledger. This allows you to know not only the total amount owed to you by all credit customers, but also the total amount owed by each customer.

Entries made in the sales and cash receipts journal are also totalled at the end of the month, and the results are posted to the accounts receivable account in your general ledger. This account is your accounts receivable "control account". What "control" means is that after all your posting is completed, the total amount of customer balances in the accounts receivable ledger will be the same as the balance in the control

Jacob W. Chikuhwa

account in the general ledger. If they are not the same, you can tell that you made an error somewhere along the line.

If you extend credit to your customers and maintain a sales and cash receipts journal by hand, look for a journal that integrates posting to the accounts receivable ledgers with the recording of sales and cash receipts transactions. This is called a "one-write" system. It will usually save you time and cut down on posting errors. If you use a computer program, posting to the accounts receivable ledgers will occur automatically.

Accounts Payable: Accounts payable are the unpaid bills of the business; the money you owe to your suppliers and other creditors. The sum of the amounts you owe to your suppliers is listed as a current liability on your balance sheet.

If you use the accrual basis of accounting, expenses are recorded in the cash disbursements journal at the time the goods or services are paid for or in the purchase journal if you buy on credit. If you deal with a given supplier many times during the month, you do not have to record every purchase. You could accumulate all bills for the month from that supplier, then record one transaction in the purchases journal at the end of the month.

You should keep an accounts payable ledger account for each supplier. Expenses from the cash disbursements journal are, at the end of each day, posted to the appropriate accounts payable ledger. The accounts payable ledger is a record of what you owe each vendor.

The general ledger contains an accounts payable account, which is your accounts payable control account. The cash disbursements journal has accounts payable credit and debit columns. Credit purchases and payments on account are entered in these two columns, respectively. At the end of the month they are totalled and posted to the control account in the general ledger.

Accounts payable ledgers will help you control your expenditures and payables. If you maintain accurate payable ledgers, it will be easy for you to double check the bills you get from your suppliers.

At the end of the month, reconcile your accounts payable ledgers with the accounts payable control account. The control account is the total accounts payable balance from your general ledger. The beginning accounts payable total, plus purchases on account during the month,

85

minus payments on account during the month, should equal the ending accounts payable total. Compare this amount to the sum of the individual accounts payable ledgers. This will help you discover any errors you made in recording your payables. Reconciliation might also help you catch any errors on vendor bills.

An accounts payable aging report is a good cash management tool that should be prepared periodically. It will help you plan the timing and amount of your cash disbursements.

The Capital Register (Asset Register): Limited companies have to keep a capital register. This records capital items they own such as land, buildings, equipment and vehicles, showing the cost at date of purchase. It also records the disposal of any of these items, and the cumulative depreciation. Movable assets should also be recorded.

The Nominal Ledger (Private Ledger): This is usually kept by your accountant or book-keeper. It brings together all the information from the 'primary' ledgers, as these other basic records are called. Expenses from the cash books and purchase ledger are 'posted' to the left-hand side of the nominal ledger. Income from sales (and any other income) is posted to the right. Normally each type of expense or income has a separate page which makes subsequent analysis an easier task.

General Ledger: The general ledger is a permanent summary of all your supporting journals, such as the sales and cash receipts journal and the cash disbursements journal. Your financial statements are built from the general ledger.

For each account title shown on your sales and cash receipts journal columns and your cash disbursements journal columns, there is a general ledger account. There are also separate general ledger accounts for miscellaneous items that do not have their own column in the journals, but are entered in a "miscellaneous" column. For example, Cash, Accounts Receivable, Accounts Payable, Sales, Purchases, Telephone Expense, and Owners Equity are all examples of general ledger accounts. There is a page reserved in the general ledger for each general ledger account.

The individual entries in the general ledger are always from the total columns of your supporting journals. When all journal entries are posted, you can arrive at the ending balance for each account. The sum

Jacob W. Chikuhwa

of all general ledger debit balances should always equal the sum of all general ledger credit balances.

Closing the Books

When you reach the end of an accounting period, you need to "close the books." At a minimum, you will close your books annually because you have to file an income tax return every year. If you are having financial statements prepared, you will want them done at least annually. However, annual financial statements may not be enough to help you keep tabs on

Even if you are not having financial statements prepared, you may want to close your books monthly. Sending out customer statements, paying your suppliers, reconciling your bank statement, and submitting sales tax reports to the State are probably some of the tasks you need to do every month. You may find it easier to do these if you close your books.

How to close your books: After you finish entering the day-to-day transactions in your journals, you are ready to "close the books" for the period. A step-by-step description of how to close the books follows. How many of the steps you do yourself depends on how much of the accounting you want to do, and how much you want to pay your accountant to do.

(i)   Post entries to the general ledger: Transfer the account totals from your journals (sales and cash receipts journal and cash disbursements journal) to your general ledger accounts.

(ii)   Total the general ledger accounts: By footing the general ledger accounts, you will arrive at a preliminary ending balance for each account.

(iii)   Prepare a preliminary trial balance: Add all of the general ledger account ending balances together. Total debits should equal total credits. This will help assure you that your accounts balance prior to making adjusting entries.

(iv)   Prepare adjusting journal entries: Certain end-of-period adjustments must be made before you can close your books. Adjusting entries are required to account for items that do not get recorded in your daily transactions. In a traditional accounting system, adjusting entries are made in a general journal.

(v) Foot the general ledger accounts again: This will give you the adjusted balance of each general ledger account.

(vi) Prepare an adjusted trial balance: Prepare another trial balance, using the adjusted balances of each general ledger account. Again, total debits must equal total credits.

(vii) Prepare financial statements: After tracking down and correcting any trial balance errors, you (or your accountant) are ready to prepare a balance sheet and income statement.

(viii) Prepare closing entries: Get your general ledger ready for the next accounting period by clearing out the revenue and expense accounts and transferring the net income or loss to owner's equity. This is done by preparing journal entries that are called closing entries in a general journal.

(ix) Prepare a post-closing trial balance: After you make closing entries, all revenue and expense accounts will have a zero balance. Prepare one more trial balance. Since all revenue and expense accounts have been closed out to zero, this trial balance will only contain balance sheet accounts. Remember that the total debit balance must equal the total credit balance. This will help ensure that all general ledger account balances are correct as of the beginning of the new accounting period.

Trial Balance: A trial balance is a list of all the nominal ledger (general ledger) accounts contained in the ledger of a business. This list will contain the name of the nominal ledger account and the value of that nominal ledger account. The value of the nominal ledger will hold either a debit balance value or a credit value balance. The debit balance values will be listed in the debit column of the trial balance and the credit value balance will be listed in the credit column. The profit and loss statement and balance sheet and other financial reports can then be produced using the ledger accounts listed on the trial balance.

The name comes from the purpose of a trial balance which is to prove that the value of all the debit value balances equal the total of all the credit value balances.

Every month, each page in the nominal ledger is totalled, and used to prepare a "trial balance". In other words, the sum of all the left-hand totals should end up equalling the sum of all the right-hand totals. This is

Jacob W. Chikuhwa

the basis of double-entry book-keeping and is what gives you confidence that the figures are correctly recorded.

Thus, the trial balance is a worksheet on which you list all your general ledger accounts and their debit or credit balance. It is a tool that is used to alert you to errors in your books. The total debits must equal the total credits. If they do not equal, you know you have an error that must be tracked down.

When closing out your books at the end of an accounting period, you will prepare three trial balances:

(i)   A preliminary trial balance is prepared using your general ledger account balances before you make adjusting entries.

(ii)   An adjusted trial balance is done after preparing adjusting entries and posting them to your general ledger. This will help ensure that the books used to prepare your financial statements are in balance.

(iii)   A post-closing trial balance is done after preparing and posting your closing entries. This trial balance, which should contain only balance sheet accounts, will help guarantee that your books are in balance for the beginning of the new accounting period.

What if your trial balance does not balance? In other words, what if total debits do not equal total credits? This should not surprise or discourage you. In fact, it might be more surprising if it **does** balance. Accounting errors happen. Even experienced book-keepers normally have to find trial balance errors.

Finding Trial Balance Errors

When preparing a trial balance, the total debits must equal the total credits (as in Table 14). Just think of the trial balance as a tool to find the errors. Use the following steps as a guide to track down the error or errors.

(i)   Be sure the numbers on your trial balance are the same numbers shown in your general ledger. Check to see if you properly classified amounts as debits or credits on your trial balance.

(ii)   Go back to your journals (sales and cash receipts journal, cash disbursements journal, and general ledger). Check that the journal totals were properly posted to the general ledger. Were

(iii)

the correct amounts posted? Were they properly classified as debits or credits?

(iv) Go back to each journal again. Look at the totals that were posted to the general ledger. Do total debits equal total credits in each journal?

(v) Go back to each journal again. Did you foot each column on each page of the journal? Did you carry forward all column totals to the next page? Did all the items entered in the "miscellaneous" column get posted to the general ledger?

(vi) Is the difference between debits and credits 1, 100, 1,000, 10,000, etc.? If so, it is probably an addition or subtraction error.

(vii) Divide the difference by two. Is the resulting number shown on your trial balance? If so, check to see if you have incorrectly classified the amount as a debit or credit.

Table 14: The Trial Balance

	Debit	Credit
Cash in bank	3,423	
Accounts receivable	11,400	
Equipment	42,900	
Accumulated depreciation, equipment		29,500
Buildings	119,000	
Accumulated depreciation building		17,950
Land	80,000	
Accounts payable		2,213

Payroll taxes payable		2,567
Mortgage payable		135,812
Capital		59,823
Drawing account	24,000	
Sales		332,462
Advertising	18,900	
Depreciation	16,760	
Insurance	4,500	
Interest expense	12,421	
Payroll taxes	16,233	
Property taxes	4,989	
Repairs and maintenance	23,430	
Utilities	3,856	
Wages	198,515	
	580,327	**580,327**

Some Book-keeping Systems

Before deciding on book-keeping systems for your business, you should take into account the size of your business, how many transactions you estimate you will create and how much time you have to invest in your record keeping. Some book-keeping systems might be:

(i)   A notebook that can be used to write in your daily transactions. This may work well for new businesses, but this book-keeping system may not be recommended to businesses that generate a lot of transactions;

(ii)   A ledger that is a preferred bookkeeping system more by accountants than a notebook. You may wish to use a ledger in addition to an accounting software program;

(iii)   A check book that may also work well for new businesses. You should make sure to separate your business check book from your personal check book;

(iv)   Microsoft Excel that can be a valuable tool in setting up a bookkeeping system. You can download a pre-written spread sheet;

(v)   A bookkeeping software program that will enable you to generate reports and financial statements with minimal effort on your part.

We will make a brief survey of some of the more 'popular' bookkeeping systems. They are divided into five categories: 'shoe boxes'; do-it-yourself books; halfway houses; accountants only; and computer-based systems.

(i)   'Shoe Box' System: This is for the simplest businesses, which need relatively little financial control beyond cash, bank accounts, accounts payable and accounts receivable. At its simplest, you need four shoe boxes, a bank paying-in book (deposit slip book), bank accounts book, a cheque book (accounts payable) and accounts receivable book (the last two can tell you how much you have in the bank). You keep two boxes for unpaid invoices (one for sales, one for purchases, services and so on). You transfer the invoices into the other two boxes (one for sales one for purchases, etc.) when each invoice is paid. By adding all the invoices in one box (sales, unpaid invoices) you can find out how much you are owed, and by adding another (purchases, unpaid) you find out how much you owe. You keep every record relating to the business, too.

This is a perfectly adequate system unless you need some form of cash control or some profit information and you need it fast. It is, however, not too good on credit control. Essentially, this system is only for the smallest firms.

Jacob W. Chikuhwa

For years, the classic approach has been a shoebox stuffed full of receipts. Today, most book-keeping software packages can retrieve your account information for your business. You can organise receipts with software to consolidate receipts for income tax reporting or warranties, and to document expense reports.

(ii) The DIY (do it yourself) System: These are normally hardback, bound books with several sections to them; each part ruled and already laid out for the entries. Each one has a set of instructions and examples for each section.

At a Glance: Few instructions, mostly related to VAT. But if you are thinking of opening a fish and chips shop they have prepared a special book-keeping ledger.

Finco Small Business Book-keeping System: Simple instructions, two years' supply of record sheets, loose-leaf. This is more easily adaptable to any business (there is less compartmentalisation), and gives detailed control over individual amounts outstanding, both receivable and payable. Because if it is loose-leaf, your accountant can take the relevant records without depriving you of your control. It can also be used in conjunction with your accountants' minicomputer.

Kalamazoo Set Up Pack: This is the most comprehensive system (as well as the most expensive). It provides everything that all other systems give you, two years supply of records (loose-leaf) and a debtors/creditors ledger.

The Kalamazoo Cash receipts System enables receipts, bank deposit and cash receipts to be written simultaneously, automatically, accurately and all in one operation. For banking, the flap of the bank deposit form supplies the permanent record of the banking transaction and can be filed for audit purposes. Transcribing errors are non-existent with this simple yet fast and accurate system.

In addition there are also the Collins Self Employed Account Book; Collins Complete Traders Account Book; Evrite Traders

Account Book; and Simplex 'D' Cash Book. All these systems mentioned here have some advantages and disadvantages in common.

The excel book-keeping spread sheets were designed from the simple small business book-keeping software used for existing clients to make financial transactions fast, easy to enter and understand. Formula driven so that minimum data is entered with automated analysis producing from the book-keeping system monthly profit and loss accounts, live debtor and creditor reports, self-assessment tax returns.

The excel book-keeping spread sheet totals each column for each book keeping month. The totals of each sheet are then collected by the accountancy software to complete the simple book keeping system by automatically producing the monthly profit and loss account and self-assessment tax return to complete the self-employed book-keeping system.

(iii) Halfway House Systems: The halfway house systems lie between a simple DIY and an 'accountant only' system. Pre-printed stationery tends to be used, but in loose-leaf form. They are more flexible than the DIY and tend to be cheaper than using an accountant only.

However, they do require some knowledge by the person who keeps the books. Again, this need not be daunting, as your accountant can probably train you (or your office girl or boy) to keep them up. The major problem is that you need your accountant before you can use your records for more advanced financial control.

There are two common halfway house systems on the market: Twinlock and Kalamazoo. At the basic level, the tow systems seem remarkably similar in financial control. Both are single-write systems (where one writing can enter up to three records).

(iv) Accountants Only Systems: The accountant only systems are those for the more complex (possibly larger) small businesses, and will be designed by your accountant. They often need trained book-keepers to run them. However, the training period can be relatively short (anything from one day upwards). The book-

Jacob W. Chikuhwa

keeper handles routine matters, and your accountant the non-routine.

As a book-keeper, one serves as the eyes and ears of the accountant, so one has to understand the basics of accounting. The book-keeper's role requires one to track all the financial transactions of a business. Accounting provides the structure which must be used to organise these transactions, as well as the procedures that must be used to record, classify, and report information about the business. On a day-to-day basis, the book-keeper makes sure that all transactions are entered accurately in the books. To be a book-keeper one must be very detail oriented and love to work with numbers, since one spends most of one's day hunched over a computer massaging the numbers.

(v)   Computer Systems: There are many small computer systems that will carry out the book-keeping and accountancy functions needed by a small business. But, like all systems, they are only as good as the quality of information put in. The other major problems with computer systems are: selecting the equipment in a market with many models with claimed advantages; making sure that you have the necessary extra equipment; making sure that you have the software (programs) capable of handling your information and record needs; and finally, ensuring that you can use the machine efficiently. This is fine for the enthusiast, but others tend to get lost in the jungle. It would certainly be safest to start off with an accounting book-keeping practice that has its own computer system.

2.6 Choosing the Form of Your Business

At the outset of your business venture, you will have to decide in what legal form to establish your business. That form will significantly influence the types of money that are available to you. There are four main forms that a business can take, with a number of variations on two of these. The form that you choose will depend on a number of factors: Commercial needs, financial risk and your tax position. All play an important part.

Financial Control

(i) Sole Trader

If you have the facilities, cash and customers, you can start trading under your own name immediately. There are no rules about the records you have to keep neither is there requirement for an external audit, or for financial information on your business to be filed with the Registrar of Companies.

You would be prudent to keep good books and to get professional advice, as you will have to declare your income to the Income Tax Department.

Without good records you will lose in any dispute over tax. You are personally liable for the debts of your business, and in the extent of your business failing, your personal possessions can be sold to meet them.

A sole trader does not have access to equity capital, which has the attraction of being risk-free to the business. He must rely on loans from banks or individuals and any other non-equity source of finance.

(ii) Partnership

There are very few restrictions to setting up in business with another person or persons in partnership. Many partnerships are formed without legal formalities, and sometimes drifted into without the parties themselves being aware that they have entered a partnership. All that is needed is for two or more people to agree to carry on a business together intending to share the profits. The law will then recognise the existence of a partnership.

Most of the points raised when considering sole tradership apply equally to partnerships. All the partners are personally liable for the debts of the business, even if those debts were incurred by one partner's mismanagement or dishonesty without the other partner's knowledge. Even death may not release a partner from his obligations, and in some circumstances his estate can remain liable. Unless you take 'public' leave of your partnership by notifying your business contacts, and advertising retirement in the Financial Gazette, you will remain liable indefinitely. So it is vital before entering a partnership to be absolutely sure of your partner and to take legal advice in drawing up a contract, which should cover the following points:

Profit Sharing, Responsibilities and Duration — this should specify how profits and losses are to be shared, and who is to carry out which

Jacob W. Chikuhwa

tasks. It should also set limits on partner's monthly drawings, and on how long the partnership itself is to last (either a specific period of years or indefinitely, with a cancellation period of, say three months).

Voting Rights and Policy Decision — unless otherwise stated, all the partners have equal voting rights. It is advisable to get a definition of what is a policy or voting decision, and how such decisions are to be made. You must also decide how to expel or admit a new partner.

Time Off — every partner is entitled to his share of the profits, even when ill or on holiday. You will need some guidelines on the length and frequency of holidays, and on what to do if someone is absent for a long period for any other reasons.

Withdrawing Capital — you have to decide how each partner's share of the capital of the business will be valued in the event of a partner leaving or the partnership being dissolved.

Accountancy Procedures — you do not have either to file accounts or to have accounts audited. However, it may be prudent to agree a satisfactory standard of accounting and have a firm of accountants to carry out that work. Sleeping partners may well insist on it.

Sleeping Partners — a partner who has put up capital but does not intend to take an active part in running the business can protect himself against risks by having his partnership registered as a limited partnership.

(iii) Limited Company

The main distinction between a limited company and either sole tradership or partnership is that it has a legal identity of its own separate from the people who own it. This means that, in the event of liquidation, creditors' claims are restricted to the assets of the company. The shareholders are not liable as individuals for the business debts beyond the paid-up value of their shares. This applies even if the shareholders are working directors, unless, the company has been trading fraudulently.

Other advantages include the freedom to raise capital by selling shares and certain tax concessions.

The disadvantages include the legal requirement for the company's accounts to be audited by a chartered or certified accountant and for certain records of the business trading activities to be filed annually with the Registrar of Companies.

A limited company can be formed by two shareholders, one of whom must be a director. A company secretary must also be appointed, who can be a shareholder, director, or an outside person such as an accountant.

The company can be bought 'off the shelf' from a registration agent then adapted to suit your own purposes. This will involve changing the name, shareholders and article of association. Alternatively, you can form your own company, using your solicitor or accountant.

(iv) Cooperative

There is an alternative form of business for people whose primary concern is to create a democratic work environment, sharing profits and control. If you want to control or substantially influence your own destiny, and make as large a capital gain out of your life's work as possible, then a cooperative is not for you.

The membership of the cooperative is the legal body that controls the business, and members must work in the business. Each member has one vote, and the cooperative must be registered under the Cooperatives Act.

There are five ways of running a successful business venture:

1. *Learn to listen* as brilliant ideas can spring from the most unlikely places. Get out there, listen to people, draw people out and learn from them. Social networking can prove useful. This can mean following online comments as closely as board meeting notes. Asking shop floor and administrative staff for their opinions can provide shrewd information.

2. You have to *do something radically different* to stand out in business. Maintain a focus upon innovation, but don't try to reinvent the wheel. A simple change for the better is far more effective than five complicated changes for the worse. There are thousands of simple business solutions to problems out there.

3. Remember your *staff are your biggest brand advocates*, and focusing on helping them and taking pride in their work will shine through in how they treat your customers. With so many different companies, nationalities and personalities running businesses, there is no shortage for competition. Businesses exist

Jacob W. Chikuhwa

in a competitive environment where there is fierce competition with each other to provide the best possible value for money for goods and services, and to offer the most suitable range of products and services for customers.

4. If you are not enjoying what you are doing in your business, you are doing it wrong. If you feel like getting up in the morning to work on your business is a chore, then it's time to try something else. If you are *having a good time*, there is a far greater chance a positive, innovative atmosphere will be nurtured and your business will flourish.

5. In time of a crisis in your business, *be adaptable* — it's one of the benefits of entrepreneurship. Every successful businessperson has experienced a few failures along the way — the important thing is how you learn from them. By being flexible and rolling with the crisis, you are able to demonstrate respect for those affected by the disruption of business activity. Create a crisis plan with your team. Having a plan with a full checklist of the many things to consider ensures that business is carried out appropriately — and with humanity. Be mindful of customers and clients in the affected areas of supply. It makes good sense for your company, your employees and your customers and clients. And in the long term, your prospects and customers will choose you over others, because you were in a position to ride over the storm. In other words, you did not allow yourself to get disheartened by a setback or two.

The high tech environment in which we do business today — with real-time tools involving email and social media — allows us to communicate and interact with millions of people in an instant with the simple click of a button, automate and pre-schedule just about anything we want to say, and carry out entire campaigns almost single handedily. These tools allow us to accomplish so much with so little — yet they can also desensitize us in a way that puts our businesses — and more importantly our humanity — at risk unless we start to pay closer attention.

PART THREE

3. DATA PROCESSING CONCEPTS

3.1 Stages in Data Processing

The Early 1960s have developed a new resource and specialisation described by such words as computer, systems, data, processing and information. Combined into expression like computer program, business systems, data processing and management information systems, data processing becomes a specialist activity concerned with the systematic recording, arranging, processing, filing and dissemination of facts relating to the physical events (transactions and other) occurring in the business.

Whereas the factory processes raw materials and produce goods for sale, a data processing department (section) processes basic data and produces basic business documents and control information for management to keep them informed of events within the business; this enables them to coordinate different activities of the organisation's functional groups and to control the day-to-day transactions and be in a position to take whatever corrective action is necessary to achieve the objectives of the particular business.

Before production can be commenced in the factory, raw materials and parts have to be procured, which involves the data processing system in the preparation of purchase orders. When supplies are received, they have to be recorded on appropriate stock or job records, which again involve data processing. The accounts of suppliers have to be updated to show the value of the goods purchased from them and the remittances made to them.

When production is due to commence, materials and parts have to be issued to the production centres and suitably recorded on issue notes which are subsequently recorded on stock and job records. The issues are often priced and extended, which are also data processing operations.

Factory employees are remunerated either for their attendance time, piecework or bonus earnings, and here the data processing system is

Jacob W. Chikuhwa

concerned with wages calculation, preparation of payslips and the collection and summarisation of data with regard to production orders or jobs.

On completion of production, the goods are despatched to customers, which involves the data processing system in the preparation of despatch documentation, invoices, sales ledger updating and the preparation of statements of account. Eventually, remittances are received from customers, which involve further data processing in respect of adjustments to the balances on customers' accounts.

The results of business transactions (operations) for specific operating periods are summarised and presented to management in the form of operating reports, profit and loss statements and balance sheets. (See Part Two.)

The production of information from data involves data processing systems that comprise of those procedures, people and machines devoted to recording and manipulating raw data. Thus, data processing is a statistical art or science in which data are processed to produce information.

Data derive most directly from business activity. They are created in the many business transactions taking place daily. Besides, data arise from the environment in which a firm operates. Knowledge of environmental characteristics like incomes, taxes, tastes and habits help a business firm to recognise and profit from market demands; actions of competitors also provide valuable information for business managers.

Like in any manufacturing (processing) plant, data processing involves certain operations whose categories are divided into seven stages (see Fig. 4):

(a) Data Capture

This is where data is originated. Figures describing a transaction or the conditions of the environment within which the organisation operates are recorded on specially designed forms known as *source documents*.

The only operation undertaken during this stage of data processing is the *recording of data*. Here transactions data are captured from an occurrence on handwritten or typed forms such as sales tickets, purchases orders, invoices, or cheques.

Data Processing Concepts

In a manual processing method, these documents are passed on to a clerk for sorting and verification before entering the data into the appropriate accounts. Business transactions are entered in chronological order into a journal. If the data are to be processed by machine (computer), they must be transcribed or converted to some machine-readable form. Increasingly, data are captured by special recording devices and entered directly into some electronic storage medium such as a magnetic tape or disk. The New Millennium has seen the emergence of the USB Mass Storage Device.

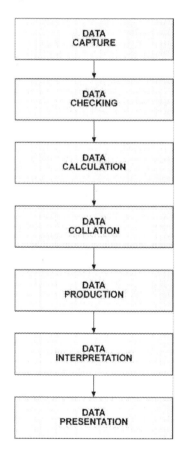

Fig. 4: Stages in Data Processing

Jacob W. Chikuhwa

(b) Data Checking

At this stage, the correctness and validity of the data recorded are ascertained and sorted. This involves the following operations:

(i)   Verification of Data — this operation entails checking or validating of data elements to ensure that they were recorded correctly.

(ii)   Classification of Data — this involves placing data elements into specific categories which provide meaning for the user, e.g. by a process known as posting, the entries in the journal are transferred to a ledger, which is a book of accounts. Each account brings together all transactions affecting one item such as cash or sales. Sales records can be classified by department, by sales person, and, perhaps, by specific item.

(iii)   Sorting of Data — this involves arranging data elements in a specified or predetermined sequence. The day's credit sales at a department store, for example, may be arranged in account-number sequence before being used to update customer account records. The processing can be more efficient when both the input file (the credit sales) and the master file (the accounts to be updated) are arranged in account-number sequence. Having both files in the same sequence makes it easier to match each transaction to the master record it affects. This results in processing efficiency.

(iv)   Controlling of Data — here, control is made to detect missing entries, illegible entries and illogical or unlikely entries.

(c) Data Calculation

This is the stage where raw materials or data are fed (input) into the processing machine (a pocket calculator or a computer). Taken from the source documents (invoices) or book of accounts (ledger) accumulated over a period e.g. a week or one month, the data are manipulated and processed and result in aggregates (assemblages) being obtained. The operations involved at this stage are:

(i)   Summarisation of Data — this involves combining or aggregating data elements in either two ways: accumulating data elements in mathematical sense or reducing data in the logical sense. The management at a department store, for instance, needs

(ii)   information on total amount of income and expenses for the whole store, for individual departments and even for individual employees in order to plan rationally.

(iii)   Processing of Data — this operation is involved with the arithmetic and/or logical manipulation of data, e.g. computations to derive averages. Data expressed in the form of averages, percentages, ratios or indices can be used to check on progress towards a goal as time passes.

(d) Data Collation

Like assembling and control of assembled (manufactured) goods, collation is done by way of reference to data already held in files or storage devices, e.g. USB device. Here, the figures are controlled and assembled in order that they are in a meaningful form. The operations involve:

(i)   Controlling of Data — control is carried out to ensure reasonableness and accuracy. This is done by comparison with previous data of a similar nature or by reference to data in files or previous monthly, quarterly, or annual reports.

(ii)   Assembling of Data — this involves placing calculated data elements into a format that can be understood by the recipient. Such formats include all *financial statements,* of which the *income statement* and the *balance sheet* are the principal ones. These are assembled at regular intervals.

(e) Data Production

This is where the end product is produced (output). The manipulation and collation of the figures are complete and a statistical analysis is produced and stored or disseminated. The operations involved at this stage are:

(i)   Analysis of Data — to reveal the full informational content of data, the underlying relationships they contain must be identified. Mere summations usually reveal little more than the symptoms of success or failure. The underlying causes of such results can only be found by examining underlying relationships. For example, the ratio of liquid assets to liabilities helps to reveal whether or not a company is able to meet its debts. Examples of

Jacob W. Chikuhwa

useful analytic tools are regression, mathematical programming and computer simulation (see Appendix I).

(ii)   Storage of Data — this implies placing of data/information into some storage media such as paper, magnetic tape, magnetic disk or microfilm or USB, where it can be retrieved when needed. This also means putting away of data/information into appropriate filing cabinets and/or computer files.

(iii)   Retrieval of Data — this operation involves the searching out and gaining access to specific data/information elements from the medium where it is stored.

(iv)   Reproduction of Data — this operation involves duplicating data/information from one medium to another or into another position in the same medium.

(f) Data Interpretation

This step in business statistics aids management to make decisions and to control operations. However, caution should be used in relying heavily on statistical measurements to influence decision making. Despite the best of intentions, several types of errors can creep into a computation. Arithmetic errors are likely to occur, particularly when the quality of data to be processed is extensive.

(g) Data Presentation

This involves showing of results in a form that is easily understood. To present statistical material in a manner that will be useful for purposes of analysis, two devices are commonly used. These are summary tables and graphic presentations. The graphic presentation of statistical data has the great advantage of presenting a visual analysis of the facts. Examples of graphic statistical presentations are the line or curve chart, the bar chart, the pie diagram or circular chart.

One is tempted to regard *dissemination of data* as an operation in its own right. However, it should be understood that the ultimate objective of data/information systems is to disseminate data/information to the final user. Facts and figures do not become information until they are received and accepted by someone with the responsibility, ability and desire to use them in decision making.

Thus, dissemination of data/information involves transferring already processed data from a device to a user in the form of a report or a display on a screen of a computer controlled terminal or indeed a monthly, or quarterly, or annual bulletin.

3.2 Nature of Business Data Processing

A business data processing system is an artificial man-made entity, which must be created, developed, implemented and managed. Like all managerial projects, it requires planning, organising, co-ordinating, controlling and staffing. The creation of a data processing system requires a combination of art, science, theory, principles, methods and practice.

Ever since human beings formed organisations, records have been kept to make possible the functioning of organisations. Whether the organisation relates to church, military, business (big or small), government, or public service, records must be kept. Hospitals must keep track of patients; banks keep financial records, savings, etc. Department stores keep track of sales and charges; post offices keep track of registered mail and packages; schools keep records of registration, grades, student loans; insurance companies keep records of policies, etc. This also involves competition and the need to minimise on expenses in order to make the business viable.

Thus, for a business firm to survive, it is obligatory that materials are purchased at the lowest possible cost, capital is invested in a prudent manner, facilities and equipment are operated with the greatest efficiency, personnel and labour are paid on a competitive scale, healthy and satisfactory working conditions are provided and high-quality products are produced, priced correctly and delivered on time. A modern business firm cannot operate just by relying on past experience; it must undergo continual change and improvement in its operations. To operate such a firm without a flexible, quick response and efficient information system, which provides data on current operations and forecasts changing conditions, would be impossible.

The principal objectives of a typical manufacturing *accounting system* are the support of the following two major business functions:

Jacob W. Chikuhwa

(i) Cost Control — all the costs involved, like labour, material inventory and transportation must be controlled and maintained at the lowest possible level.

(ii) Operational Control — to survive and remain competitive, a manufacturing firm must maintain an efficient and high-level utilisation of equipment, keep a well-planned production schedule, have quick inventory turnover, high space utilisation, prompt customer service, immediate elimination of obsolescent products and quick design of new products.

It is pertinent to note that a typical manufacturing accounting system should contain the following subsystems:

(i) Order entry and invoicing/billing;
(ii) Payroll;
(iii) Product definition and costing;
(iv) Sales analysis;
(v) Accounts payable;
(vi) Accounts receivable;
(vii) General Ledger;
(viii) Inventory management;
(ix) Production status and costing;
(x) Business systems audit and review.

The manufacturing accounting information system shown in Table 15 is a subsystem of a manufacturing system, which, in turn, is a subsystem of a corporate organisation. The business systems approach looks at the whole and focuses on the fact that the manufacturing accounting information system must operate in the environment of the corporation.

It is necessary to note that the accounting information system has a mechanical structure. The basis of the mechanical structure, as in all business data processing systems, is the concept of a *file*.

A file is a set of records relating to a specific business activity. An example of a file is the accounts receivable file (Table 15, vi). At a department store, for instance, it is made up of the individual records for the credit (charge) customers of the store. Each individual record shows, basically, the amount of money that a customer owes the store. Each record may also contain some or all of the following facts for a customer:

(i) Name and address

(ii) Credit standing or credit limit

(iii) Date of the last payment

(iv) Details on unpaid credit transactions (dates, items purchased, prices and costs, etc.)

(v) Customer's employers and monthly salary

The basic accounts receivable file just described is the *master file* of the accounts receivable system. Customer transactions (purchases or payments) are recorded in a *transaction file* and used to update the records in the master file. Other changes to the master file are recorded in a *change file* and made as well. Records for departing customers must be purged from the file (the records must be closed out and withdrawn from the file). Poor credit risks must also be purged. Customer records change as customers marry, lose family members in death, change address, change credit status, etc. It is clear then that a master file is created; then transactions and changes are recorded and used to change the master file to keep it current.

Obviously, various reports must be created by the system. Management must know the amount and rate of default (uncollectable) on credit sales. They must also know the volume of such sales in total and by department, etc. These reports are created from the transactions, the changes and the updated master file.

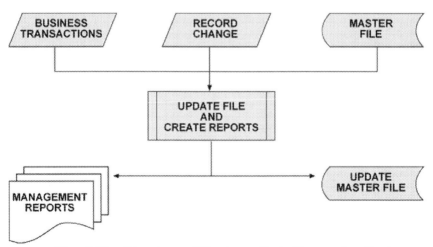

Fig. 5 The Structure of Business Data Processing Systems

Jacob W. Chikuhwa

As shown in Fig. 5 above, a business data processing system is created and operated by developing a master file and a system for updating it as transactions and changes that effect its contents occur. Management reports are developed from the flow of transactions and changes affecting the master file and from the updated master file itself.

Table 15: Structure of the Manufacturing Accounting System

SUBSYSTEMS	FUNCTIONS	OUTPUTS/DOCUMENTS
1	2	3
i) ORDER ENTRY AND		Order entry/change list, order acknowledgement, item price list,
INVOICING/BILLING	Order entry	picking list
INPUT:	Invoicing/billing	Order release list, invoice register, invoice
Customer orders	Order status	Open order by customer, order status by item, open order status in date sequence
ii) PAYROLL	Payroll processing	Payroll input audit listing, current hours proof, gross earnings register, payroll register, payroll cheques year-to-date/quarter-to-date earnings register, employee miscellaneous deduction register, vacation/holiday/sick hour register, payroll distribution journal
INPUTS: Time sheets, general data collection system	National and provincial Reporting	Employee register, e. g. PAYE register/(PAYE = pay as you earn)
Support reports	Union reporting	Fixed union register, union consolidation register, local union report
	Miscellaneous reporting	Labour distribution register, job distribution register, workers' compensation work sheet, cheque reconciliation register
iii) PRODUCTION	Parts list	Single-level parts list, indented parts list, summarised parts list
DEFINITION AND COSTING	Where-used list	Single-level where-used item — final assembly where-used
INPUTS: Assembly drawings, cost records, inventory management	Product cost reports	Single-level parts list standard cost, indented parts list standard cost, product cost report, product cost report simulation

1	2	3
system outputs		
iv) SALES ANALYSIS	Salesperson sales analysis	Daily salesperson recap, sales analysis by salesperson, profit analysis by salesperson
INPUTS: Outputs of a) order entry and invoicing/ billing; b) inventory management; c) accounts receivable subsystem	Item sales analysis	Sales analysis by item, profit analysis by item
v) ACCOUNTS PAYABLE	Invoice processing	Purchase journal proof, purchase journal
	Payment processing	Cash requirements report, cash disbursement journal, accounts payable cheques
INPUTS: Credit memos, prepaid cheques,	Management reporting	Open payables by due dates, open payables listing, vendor analysis report
vendor invoices, bank statements	Cheque reconciliation	Cheque reconciliation register
vi) ACCOUNTS RECEIVABLE	Daily processing	Transaction entry/change, cash receipts/adjustment register, invoice transaction register
INPUTS: Invoice summaries,	Account status	Customer account status report, paid open item proof
cash receipts, adjustments	Monthly processing	Aged trial balance, statements, delinquency notice
vii) GENERAL LEDGER	Journal entry processing	General journal report, general journal
INPUTS: General journals	Monthly processing	Financial statement work-sheet, general ledger monthly audit listing, general ledger, general ledger listing, statement of income, balance sheet
	Annual processing	Fiscal year-end audit listing, statement of income, balance sheet
viii) INVENTORY MANAGEMENT INPUTS:	Inventory transaction processing	Transaction entry/change, inventory transaction register

1	2	3
Orders, issues, receipts, adjustments, allocations	Inventory status	Month-end inventory stock status, inventory stock status review, inventory reorder report, physical inventory list
	Order status	On-order report by item, on-order report by vendor, on-order report by date
	Inventory management analysis	Inventory analysis report, inventory valuation and variance, A-B-C analysis report
ix) PRODUCTION STATUS	Job master information	Basic item summary list, maintenance work sheet
AND COSTING	Job release and update	Open job release summary, job work sheet, labour tickets, job transaction edit register, job update register
INPUTS: Outputs of		
a) payroll b) accounts payable	Shop cost reports	Projection work sheet, accounting job summary, job cost analysis report, accounting job closeout
c) inventory management subsystems. job tickets, general	Shop production reports	Work list report, production job summary, production status report, production job closeout
data collection system support reports		
x) BUSINESS SYSTEMS	Audit/review inception	Management/steering committee assignment brief
AUDIT AND REVIEW	Audit/review status	Audit/review statement by systems analyst, audit/review status by subsystem, audit/review status in date sequence
INPUTS: Formal reports, flowcharts,	Systems performance analysis	Systems analysis (audit) report — evaluating system performance, system analysis (audit) report — advancing modifications and improvements
interview and observation	Management and corporate social audit	Statement on personnel turnover and general performance, statement on
documentation		firm's impact on society

Like any system, a business data processing system is created and operated for a purpose. In other words, it is an organised endeavour with one or more definite objectives in mind. The reasons for capturing the facts associated with business transactions and processing them can be grouped in three general categories:

Data Processing Concepts

(i)   Management Planning and Control Activities — management must plan for future activity and exercise control over current activity if plans are to be carried out successfully. Such actions determine the profitability (success) of the enterprise. If we are to take a department store as an example; the management of the department store must know if actual sales are below, equal to, or above expected sales. Inventory amounts (number of suits by size, colour and style) must be adjusted to actual sales. If, in another department of the store, fewer suits are being sold than anticipated, unsold suits will remain in stock. Prices (and profit margins) may have to be reduced in order to move the suits out to make room for faster-selling items. If sales are equal to expectations, then the suits purchased can all be sold, and future orders can continue at planned levels. In other words, the same plan of action can continue because it is successful.

Obviously, if actual sales are above expected sales, adjustments in plans are called for. The number of suits ordered has not satisfied customer demands; therefore; plans need to be modified and the pace of orders stepped up. It should even be that more salespersons, stock clerks and tailors are required to handle the increased sales.

(ii) Basis for Custodial (Maintenance) Processing — just as the buildings, furnishings and heating systems of an organisation must be taken care of, documents (sales slips, paycheques, purchase orders, receiving slips, tax reports, etc.) must be prepared and their contents recorded, manipulated and compared in order to carry on the daily business routine. Employees must be paid and customers must be billed. Purchase orders must be prepared to obtain supplies for the enterprise and supplier invoices must be recorded for payment as goods are received. Legal reporting requirements (income tax reports, health reports on employees handling food, etc.) must be met if the enterprise is not to be forced to close down. Such activities are necessary to continued operation, although they may contribute only indirectly to profit (success).

Jacob W. Chikuhwa

> Data generated by transactions and contained on custodial documents may serve as the basis for information reports to management; but the processing necessary to their production and use (completing a purchase order, for example), although required to keep the operation going, is not a basic planning or control activity of management.

(iii) Provision of Historical Facts — planning cannot be rational without historical data to use in establishing past and current trends and tendencies. Furthermore, adequate management control of any activity requires the recognition of performance standards. Such standards are most often obtained from the analysis of past (historical) behaviour. Legal requirements exist for retaining past data as a basis for tax and other reports.

It is essential to note that the three reasons for data processing are listed in the order of their relative importance. The most important use of business data is in providing management with the information necessary to recognise trends and patterns in the activities of the enterprise and in the environment within which it operates. However, emphasis on management information does not really come at the expense of the other needs for data processing. A data processing system that collects and preserves the proper facts to provide adequate information for management planning and control will, of necessity, perform the custodial processing required to keep the enterprise in operation. Nevertheless, a system designed primarily for efficient custodial processing may not necessarily provide good management information. The custodial approach tends to put major emphasis on reducing the cost of inescapable processing activities. Putting management information needs first, emphasises the importance of considering profit motives when striving for improvement in data processing procedures.

The characteristics of an effective data processing system are the need for the system to be timely, pertinent, precise and accurate and economically feasible and efficient.

(i) A timely data processing system will capture current data and output current information. For example, the department store manager who receives an analysis of departmental sales for the previous quarter one month after the close of that quarter is reacting to situations that may very well have changed dramatically since the quarter ended. Timely processing that reflects current conditions can help a manager perform his duties effective and efficient enough to be able to nip any problems in the bud.

Ideally, data should be processed into information fast enough to provide adequate control of the physical operation that generated the data. In such a case, information is fed back in time to affect the situation from which the raw data were generated. Such a data processing system is called a real-time data processing system.

(ii)   A pertinent data processing system will provide the proper information and do the proper custodial processing. A system for evaluating performance for the shoe department in our mythical department store should not be overly concerned with reporting the colour of each pair of shoes sold. It should, however, attempt to capture data concerning the extent to which customers found shoes in the colours they wanted i.e. the reasons why potential customers were not served. On the other hand, the manager of the shoe department need not receive personnel performance reports relating to the personnel in the clothing department.

(iii)   The terms precise and accurate refer to two aspects of what people ordinarily think of as accuracy (correct values). A precise value, for our purpose, is correct within the limits of allowable error. For example, the manager of our department store does not need to know that total sales in the notions department this year were exactly $125 235.79; he would probably remember this figure as $125 000. For the manager's purpose, the $125 000 figure may be sufficiently precise, sufficiently close to the exact value. Just how precise and accurate management information has to be depends on how the information is to be used. For planning purposes, it is definitely important that information be accurate, but it does not have to be absolutely precise. In controlling detailed operations at the department level, however, information must be both very precise and very accurate.

Jacob W. Chikuhwa

(iv)   To be economically feasible and efficient, a data processing system must do two things: (a) it must not place an excessive burden on the physical operation generating the data to be processed and (b) it must give the most information possible for the dollars expended. The latter statement implies that it would not be possible to change an efficient system to get more information without spending more money. The former is more complex. If processing costs are too high, the physical operation will eventually have to cease. However, just the fact that the returns from the physical operation are sufficient to cover the associated processing costs does not mean that the level of processing is appropriate.

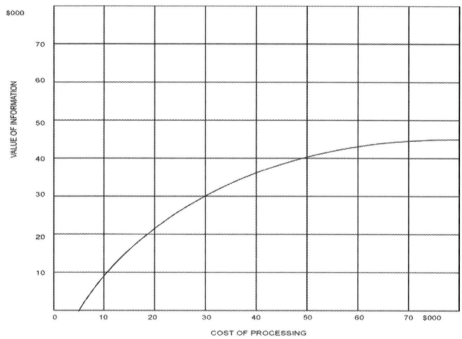

Fig. 6: Relationship of the Cost of Processing and the Value of Information

The general relationship between cost and value of processing is shown in Fig. 6. This is an application of the principle of *diminishing returns*. As cost of processing increases, the value of the information received for each dollar of expense tends to increase, but at a rapidly decreasing rate. Eventually, very little additional information is being obtained for each addition to processing costs. Ideally, investment in the process is stopped at the point where the value of the last unit of information generated is just equal to the cost of obtaining it.

3.3 Centralised vs. Distributed data Processing

Centralised Data Processing

When a business comprises of only one factory or office as opposed to a group of factories or other business units, then a centralised data processing system would be appropriate. If a corporation has many branches, as more or less all large corporations are, a centralised data processing system may not be the best for the total situation. Even if the centralised data processing system utilises all the data processing resources most effectively, the combined resources of the corporation may not be used in the best possible manner.

If a computer is implemented for the purpose of centralised data processing, the way it is used requires careful consideration. Sometimes the computer may only be used for processing routine accounting applications such as payroll, sales ledger, stock control, purchase ledger, etc.

To obtain the maximum benefit, however, the computer should be used to aid management in problem-solving and decision-making by the use of quantitative application packages for linear programming, statistical stock control, production planning, net-work analysis, discounted cash flow, etc. (for some of these, see Appendix I). When a computer is used for all the functions within the business, it is a centralised facility in the form of a data processing and information system.

To obtain the maximum benefit, however, the computer should be used to aid management in problem-solving and decision-making by the use of quantitative application packages for linear programming, statistical stock control, production planning, net-work analysis,

Jacob W. Chikuhwa

discounted cash flow, etc. (for some of these, see Appendix I). When a computer is used for all the functions within the business, it is a centralised facility in the form of a data processing and information system.

When a business organisation is a widely dispersed conglomeration of various types of operating units, including factories, warehouses and sales outlets and offices and a computer is in use, it is usually located at the head office of the group. In these circumstances, the objective would be to provide the best possible service for the data processing and information needs of all functions of all functions and operating units in the group.

The benefit to be derived from a centralised service may be summarised as follows:

(i)   Economy of capital expenditure due to the high cost of mainframe computers through having only one mainframe computer for use by the group instead of several located in the various units.

(ii)   If one large powerful computer is implemented, the resultant advantages are: increased speed of operation, storage capacity and processing capability.

(iv)   Economy in computer operating costs due to the centralisation of systems analysts, programmers, computer operators and other data processing staff as compared with the level of costs that would be incurred if each unit in the group had its own computer on a decentralised basis, i.e. avoiding the duplication of resources.

(v)   Centralisation would also facilitate the standardisation of applications, but this would depend upon the extent of diversity in the dispersed operations regarding payroll and invoicing structures, etc.

While centralised data processing managers tend to neglect the human factor and the special personal needs of local users, there are economic factors that militate in its favour. The advantages also include economy for personnel, ease in enforcing standards, and security.

If the computer is also communications oriented, whereby all operating units are equipped with transmission terminals such as visual display units (VDUs) connected to the central computer, then basic data may be speedily transmitted back and printed on a local printer. This would reduce any time delay in receiving computer output through the post or messenger service. The possibility of an integrated management information system then becomes feasible, as data from dispersed units is speedily processed for local use and information becomes available at head office by means of the computer files for corporate planning.

Such a centralised computing service should be structured in the organisation at a level which enables the data processing manager to report to a higher level of management than the departmental level or functional level for which he is providing a service. This enables policy matters to be established at Board level, rather than at functional level, which establishes the use of the computer on a corporate strategic basis in order to optimise its use. If the data processing manager reports to the managing director, he is free from direct inter-functional conflict as problems are resolved at a higher level.

Distributed Data Processing

For a multi-location corporation with far-flung operations, decentralisation is inevitable, and so the issue of distributed data processing must always be raised.

Distributed data processing must not be confused with decentralised data processing, even though decentralisation is a feature of distributed data processing. Prior to the advent of the computer, different companies in a group may well have used their own data processing installation, i.e. a decentralised facility. The centralisation of data processing was the trend of the 1960s, but the tendency of the new millennium has been a reversal of this situation, largely due to the development of mini- and micro-computers. These computers cost much less than mainframes, which makes it a viable proposition to install them in departments and branches on a distributed data processing basis. This is the philosophy of providing computer power where it is most needed, instead of concentrating all processing in a single centralised computer system.

A distributed data processing network would be designed on the basis of a philosophy whereby small computers in dispersed operating units may be connected by a communications network to each other and also to a large, centrally-located mainframe. The mainframe may support a

Jacob W. Chikuhwa

large database, which would allow information of a strategic nature to be retrieved on demand for corporate planning.

The mini- and micro-computers may be *dedicated machines* being used for a single main purpose and, in some instances, may be used as stand-alone processing systems when appropriate. This situation allows a high degree of autonomy at the local operating level which encourages motivation, flexibility and a greater acceptance of responsibility by the local management.

Simplicity of gaining access to the computer by relevant operating personnel at all levels of an organisation is not an easy matter to accomplish even with a single organisation equipped with terminals. This problem is accentuated when there are many dispersed units within the organisation, many of which may be inter-dependent, e.g. marketing and manufacturing functions, as all units must be fully aware of the operational status of each other's sphere of operations.

It becomes even more of a problem when a business is a multinational organisation with widely-dispersed subsidiaries. With the implementation of distributed data processing systems, this is not so much of a problem because it is of no consequence whether the small computers are located in the same building as a mainframe computer or whether they are situated the other side of the oceans. Distributed data processing allows a business to select the level of processing autonomy in respect of depots, factories, warehouses or sales outlets and offices.

Distributed data processing also includes the use, on a decentralised basis, of intelligent terminals, i.e. terminals with processing capabilities which may be used locally for off-line operations or for on-line operations linked to a host computer.

Furthermore, distributed data processing is located close to the user and responsibility is with local managers. Thus, there is pressure to become more tolerant and friendly to the user. In other words, distributed data processing tends to be more responsive to the needs of users, more adaptable to change and more suitable to growth.

It must be recognised that there are various degrees of distributed data processing. For example, some organisational units may be so independent of other units that stand-alone data processing becomes the most suitable method of operation. And yet other data processing tasks are so large or so interrelated with other tasks that they cannot be performed except on large central computer systems. To clarify the levels of distribution of data processing power, it is necessary to distinguish among three levels of distributed data processing:

(i)   Low Level of Distribution — in such a system only data entry and inquiry is performed locally and all data processing is done centrally by the host computer. This is accomplished by using intelligent terminals. Such systems result in more reliable data because data editing, correction, file checking, etc. can be done locally. Also local management is given more control over what data to enter and provided with improved inquiry capability.

(ii)   Intermediate Level of Distribution — in these systems there is a local base on floppy disks/diskettes and the capability of processing this local *database* through intelligent terminals and mini-computers. Thus, local management can generate reports to control day-to-day operations and can schedule data processing operations locally. Often also the capability of entering remote batch processing tasks to the host computer is provided. It is pertinent to note that at this level of distribution probably no data processing professional would be employed locally, so technical analysis, systems analysis and programming would be provided by the central staff of the host computer installation.

(iii)   High Level of Distribution — at this level of sophistication, several computers are connected and operate in a co-ordinated and co-operative manner. There is communication from host to local, from local to host, and from local to local or peer to peer computers. There are local databases and local data processing. If there is a need, the computers can combine and form effectively larger computer systems and perform large data processing tasks. Thus, dynamic and flexible data processing configurations can be created, depending on the job at hand. Data and other resources can be shared, and data processing is distributed among the various tasks of the different computers. Processing is always done where it is most economical and by the best combination of resources. The host computer has the largest staff of data processing professionals and assists other

Jacob W. Chikuhwa

> computer staffs in developing systems to be used locally. Thus, at this level of sophistication we have the two worlds of centralised and decentralised data processing systems blended by keeping the advantage of both systems and eliminating the weaknesses of each.

3.4 Concept of a Database

A Database Management System (DBMS) is a set of computer programs that controls the creation, maintenance, and the use of a database. It allows organizations to place control of database development in the hands of data administrators (DBAs) and other specialists. This DBMS is a system of software package that helps the use of integrated collection of data records and files known as databases. It allows different user application programs to easily access the same database. A DBMS also provides the ability to logically present database information to users.

As mentioned above, separate departments may have their own separate data processing systems and collect their own input for processing with the result that they have their own separate data files. The accounting data files are set up to suit the preparation of financial accounts; the marketing data files, the preparation of production schedules and the monitoring of inventory levels. These files frequently contain duplicate data about customers, employees and products.

In contrast, the database concept requires the use of some form of general data storage. The organisation's data must be stored in such a way that the same data can be accessed by multiple users for varied applications. This can be accomplished by using a database, which groups, or structures, data elements to fit the information needs of an entire organisation rather than specially for one application or functional area (group). Thus, multiple departments can use the data, and duplication of files is avoided.

In addition to reducing redundancy and increasing data independence, the database increases efficiency. When a particular item is to be updated, the change needs to be made only once. There is no need for multiple updates as required with separate files. The integration of data also permits the results of updating to be available to the entire organisation at the same time. Furthermore, the database concept provides flexibility because the system can respond to information requests that previously may have had to bridge several departments' individual data files.

It is pertinent to note that the designing of data for a database is approached from two perspectives:

(i)   Physical Design — this refers to how the data is kept on storage devices and how it is accessed.

(ii)   Logical Design — this deals with how data is viewed by application programs or individual users.

The logical data design is performed by the systems analyst and data analyst. Together, they attempt to model the actual relationships that exist among data items. Logical records should be designed independent of physical storage considerations. The physical design is often performed by the database administration (DBA) team. Taking into account such problems as data redundancy, access time and storage constraints, this team tries to implement the logical data design within the physical records and files actually stored in the database.

A logical unit can extend across more than one physical file. That is to say, what one user views as a logical unit of data may include data from the employee file and the payroll file. Conversely, one physical file may contain parts of several logical units of data. One user's logical unit may include only an employee's name and address; another may include the employee's number and job code. In both cases, the data is only a part of one physical file: the employee file. Generally speaking, the principle "an output from one system (subsystem) may be an input for another", should be observed when structuring a database.

Fig. 7 illustrates a situation where redundancy is created as the same data elements in each of the files are updated separately. The personnel system, for instance, maintains a file of employee records containing data elements in respect of employee name, address, number, marital status, department number, grade and rate of pay, etc. Similar data elements are also stored in the payroll system used in the preparation of wages and maintaining a record of earnings and tax. An input of current

Jacob W. Chikuhwa

transaction data is required to each application to update relevant data elements.

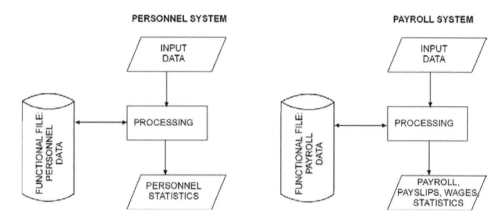

Fig. 7: Functional (Subsystem) Approach to File Structures

When separate files are maintained with common data elements, some are out of phase with others, which is due either to different updating cycles or frequencies or even omitting to update a file completely.

The use of a database should be accomplished by the following factors:

(i)   Data should be input once only.
(ii)   Redundant data should be eliminated.
(iii)   Data should be capable of being speedily retrieved.
(iv)   Files should be easy to maintain.
(v)   Files should be expandable.
(vi)   Access to files should be restricted to authorised users by the use of passwords.
(vii)   Restart and recovery procedures are necessary.
(viii) Selective print-outs should be provided for the specific information requirements of managers.

Fig. 8, on the other hand, illustrates that a database system aims at eliminating such duplication of storage and updating and providing the means for retrieving data elements for each of the application requirements in the required combinations. All data relating to a specific

Data Processing Concepts

subject, employees in this case, is then consolidated rather than fragmented within several functional files.

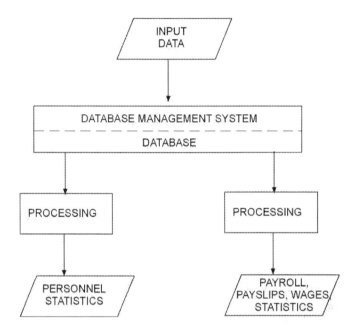

Fig. 8: Database Approach to File Structures — Integrated Files

(ix)   Provision should be made for batch and on-line processing.
(x)   New data structures should be capable of being incorporated into the database.
(xi)   Distinction should be made between the physical and the logical storage of data.
(xii) Should be capable of contending with changing circumstances within the business.
(xiii) The cost of storing data should be optimised.
(xiv) Should be self-monitoring including the provision of audit trails.

One of the problems of setting up a database for systems integration purposes is the classification of data elements as each must be allocated a data name for identification purposes. Data elements may be known by different names in the various functions and a data classification scheme is therefore essential before a database can be got off the ground. A data

Jacob W. Chikuhwa

dictionary (DD) consisting of data definitions, characteristics and inter-relationships is therefore very necessary.

A data dictionary can be defined as a store holding information that describes and specifies the characteristics of each piece of data used in a system. In other words it is an electronic glossary defining each of the data items incorporated in the whole system. A DD may also include definitive descriptions of processing within the system.

The main point about having a DD is that experience has shown over and over again that data easily becomes ambiguous. People are inclined to give different names to the same thing, and the same name to two or more different things. For example, one person may refer to the "stock number" and another person calls it the "commodity code". Similarly programmers are apt to employ different names for the same data item in their programs, e. g. STKNO and COMCDE.

A DD attempts to obviate these problems by pinning data down according to clear definitions. Each piece of data has the following characteristics ascribed to it:

(i)   Name — meaningful, standardised and preferably constructed in a program-defined form such as in COBAL, e.g. STOCK-NO.

(ii)   Description — a brief explanation of the meaning of the data item.

(iii) Aliases — a list of alternative names that have been used for the data item.

(iv)   Related data — it may be useful to draw attention to data that is closely connected with or has a similar name to the data item although it is not an alias, e.g. VAT status and VAT rate.

(v)   Range of Values — a data item may have a continuous range of values, in which case only its maximum and minimum values are included. Alternatively, the values may be discrete, e.g. discount rates of 0%, 10% and 20% only, or one fixed value, e.g. a fixed price. The other possibility is a coded value, e.g. 10 = Harare, 11 = Mutare, and so on.

(vi)   Layout — this is the "picture" of the data item as it exists outside the computer and so is conveniently specified and held in the form that is distinctly different to prevent errors caused by identical code numbers appearing in different sets, e.g. a manufactured component with code number 4505 could become confused with a finished product whose code is also 4505.

(vii)   Encoding — an indication of the form in which the data is encoded, e. g.

1 = binary, 2 = ASCII, 3 = EBDIC, etc.

(viii)   Editing — a specification of any editing or special checks that the data item must undergo, especially on input.

Data dictionaries come in a variety of types, some are stand-alone, others relate to a certain database management system (DBMS). Small data dictionaries of up to a few hundred items can be maintained manually using a card index system. Larger dictionaries are automated, generally through the employment of a data dictionary package. An automated dictionary has the advantage of being able to provide a variety of useful listings and reports. Examples are a full alphabetic list of all items, a selected list based on the first few letters of the name, a search facility for letter groups, e.g. to find items whose names are not completely known.

The work of creating and maintaining the DD falls upon the database administrator.

Database Management Systems (DBMS)

To facilitate the use of a database, an organisation can use a database management system (DBMS) — a set of programs that serves as the major interface between the database and its three principal users: the programmer, the operating system and the user. By purchasing an available DBMS, an organisation greatly reduces the need to develop its own detailed data–handling software.

One of the major purposes of a DBMS is to effect the physical data independence. This permits the physical layout of data files to be altered without necessitating changes in application programs. Such insulation between a program and the data with which it interacts is extremely desirable. The programmer does not have to pay attention to the physical nature of the file. He can simply refer to the specific data that the program needs.

Most existing DBMS provide the following facilities:

(i)   Integration of the data into logical structures that model the actual relationships among data items.

Jacob W. Chikuhwa

Provision for storing the volume of data required to meet the needs of multiple users.

(ii) Provision for concurrent retrieval and updating of data.

(iii) Methods of arranging data to eliminate duplication and thereby avoid inconsistencies that arise from duplication.

(iv) Provision for privacy controls to prevent unauthorised access to data.

(v) Controls to prevent unintended interaction or interference among programs that run concurrently.

(vi) Capability for database interface from within application programs coded in high-level programming languages.

It is interesting to note that recently the use of prewritten application software packages has increased dramatically. This increase can be attributed largely to two factors: (a) the increased cost of developing application software and (b) the rise in popularity of micro-computers. For medium to large computers, the costs associated with developing and maintaining application software have become a very significant cost of doing business; one that can be reduced by purchasing prewritten software packages. In the case of micro-computer users, many would be forced to write application software themselves or to hire programmers to do it for them if application software packages were not already available. The availability of these packages, therefore, provides businesses and computer users with an alternative means of acquiring application software.

In our discussion of database management systems, it is significant to look at data-management packages (software). Usually known as *data managers*, data-management packages are application software packages that computerise the everyday tasks of recording and filing information. The traditional manual filing system, using pencil, paper, file folders and file cabinets, is replaced by a computer system where data managers are used. Data is recorded using a computer terminal and keyboard and is stored in the computer's secondary storage devices where it can be accessed.

Most data-management packages contain a number of standard features, including the following:

(i) The ability to add or delete information within a file.

Data Processing Concepts

The ability to search a file for information based on some criterion.

(ii)   The ability to update information within a file.

(iii)   Sorting of information into some order.

(iv)   The ability to print reports or even mailing labels.

There are, however, two types of data managers, and although many of the standard functions mentioned above are contained in both types, the two types differ greatly in their capabilities. The two types of data managers are file handlers and database packages.

File handlers and database packages differ mostly in the way in which the data is stored and hence how it can be accessed. File handlers were developed earlier than database packages and were designed to duplicate the traditional manual methods of filing. Before the use of computers for filing, sections or departments in a business generally kept records that pertained only to their particular area of interest. The payroll department, for example, might keep an employee's name, address, number, salary and number of deductions to facilitate the writing of paycheques/slips. The personnel department, on the other hand, might keep each employee's name. Each department would keep its own information independently for its own use.

The cluster file handler mechanism makes it possible to store, retrieve, rename, delete, etc. files using the database. The following file handlers are known to the system by default:

- eZ FS File Handler — This is the default file handler which makes it possible to use the file system when dealing with files.
- eZ FS2 File Handler – This is the enhanced standard file handler, with better concurrency handling. It requires linux or PHP 5.3 on windows, and was still considered experimental.
- eZ DB File Handler – This is the database file handler. It makes it possible to use the database when dealing with files (in a cluster environment, this would typically be images, uploaded binary files and content-related caches, etc.). It is split into different back-ends that are compatible with the supported database engines.
- Currently supported databases for this file handler are MySQL and Oracle (when using the eZOracle extension).

Jacob W. Chikuhwa

- eZ DFS File Handler – This is the Distributed File System handler with a DB overlay. This handler is required for NFS-based architectures. It clusters by storing the cluster files mainly on NFS (the distributed file system), while the file metadata (size, mtime, expiry status) are maintained in a database table similar to the one used by eZ DB file handler. NFS is used to read and write the reference copy of clustered files.

Computers and computerised record-keeping made it possible for the procedures and methods of recording and filing data to be converted from paper, file folders and file cabinets to computer software and storage devices. Computer access allows each department to maintain its own independent files. The personnel department would have access to the employee file, while the payroll department would have access to the payroll file.

File handlers, therefore, can access only one data file at a time. They also cause duplication of data between files when used in a situation where many files containing similar information must be maintained — as often happens in a large corporation. This is not to say, however, that file handlers are not useful in certain situations. A small business, for example, can benefit greatly from the use of a file handler package that helps to organise and properly maintain the business's inventory.

File handling software did have some drawbacks for companies that had enormous amounts of data and limited computer resources. Because of the duplication of data and difficulty in accurately keeping one piece of information, such as an employee address, across several files, large companies began to develop databases. As shown above, databases consolidate various independent files into one integrated whole from which all users can have access to the information they need. Such consolidation means that a piece of data needs to be located in only one place, making it easier to maintain (see Fig. 8). Users can still search for, update, add, or delete data as with a file handler; it is the way in which the data is organised and stored that differs.

Data managers have a number of uses in the home, in business and in specialised situations. Data managers, file handlers in particular, have proven to be very popular software packages for use in the home. They can be used for such things as creating a computerised Christmas card list, compiling a computerised recipe index card file and balancing the chequebook. The data manager software package can be used for just about any type of record keeping and filing done in the home.

Other possible uses of data managers in the home include: keeping a person-property inventory, creating a listing of important documents and their locations, keeping a computerised address book and phone listing, creating a mailing list, keeping an appointment calendar and keeping track of works within a personal library. File handlers simply offer a means of computerising a manual record-keeping task — that of keeping organised, readily accessible records.

File handlers are also popular with small businesses that can benefit from the conversion of manual record-keeping processes to computerised record keeping. This process of converting manual filing systems to computerised filing systems has been possibly the greatest single use of data managers. Any aspect of a business that uses some form of file system, such as rolodex file or file cabinet, could potentially be computerised using a data manager. Business systems (applications) that are easily adapted to the use of a data manager include the keeping of employee records, inventory control and listing of suppliers and customers.

Some examples of database packages are:

- One of the most commonly used database systems is MySQL. MySQL is actively behind the scenes at Facebook, Flickr, Youtube and WordPress. If you have ever visited any of these sites, you are already familiar with the impressive results of database software and how it organizes vast amounts of information into an easy-to-digest format.

- SQL Packager scripts and compresses both the data and schema of a database into a deliverable .exe file. Its highly customizable options enable you to generate package scripts to exactly fit your needs. Installing, updating, or distributing your database can be done quickly and easily. SQL Packager also makes it easy to archive your database, and is an excellent solution for making a backup of your database when you don't have SQL Server administration rights.

Jacob W. Chikuhwa

- RPM Package Manager is a package management system. The name RPM refers to two things: software packaged in the RPM file format, and the package manager itself.
- The celebrated QuickBooks 2008 range of bookkeeping software packages is comprised of QuickBooks SimpleStart, QuickBooks Pro and QuickBooks Premier. Each one of these software programs is a comprehensive accounting system in its own right.
- Accountsdialog is an application to view and modify user accounts information.

Database management software is sold in pieces as well as in entire systems. The user can purchase only data-access languages or data-dictionary languages (data definition languages) or even file maintenance packages. Total DBMS systems combining the three elements of data definition, database maintenance and database access are becoming more common, however. These systems are usually sold separately as add-ons to a specific operating system. The most widely used complete database management systems are TOTAL (Cincom Systems Inc. IMS (IBM), ADABAS (Software AG) and IDMS (Cullinane Corporation), ERP (Hansa World) Oracle 9i Database, etc. (For a list of current software, go to www.wikipedia.org)

3.5 Careers in Data Processing

The incidence of data processing in an organisation depends upon a number of factors, among which are the size of the business, the volume of data to be processed, the dispersion of operating units and the information needs of the various functions and departments of the business. In general, as volumes of data for processing increase, it becomes necessary to consider the introduction of a data processing department which would make use of mechanised or computerised methods of data processing.

Thus, data processing is a specialist activity consisting of different areas of technical specialisation. As with other departments, data processing departments' structures and staff compliments vary from company to company. The size of this department has a general

Data Processing Concepts

relationship to the size of the company, but also reflects the complexity of the company's operations.

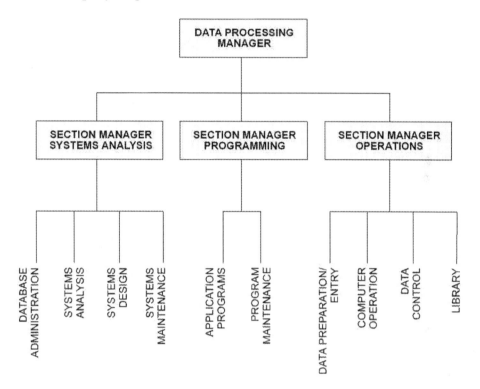

Fig. 9: Organisation Chart of a Data Processing Department

In broad terms, a largish data processing department is subdivided into systems, programming and operations, as shown in Fig. 9. The dividing line between systems and programming is not quite clear and the two functions are sometimes merged into one.

It is also possible that systems is seen as a function outside the orbit of the data processing department, perhaps as a department in its own right or part of a management services function. Another possibility is where the system analysts are on the staff of user departments, either on a temporary basis or permanently. This arrangement has the advantage of keeping the systems analysts close to the actual work going on.

Jacob W. Chikuhwa

A problem that sometimes arises, and may do so more in the future, is the career structure of programmers. As more packaged software becomes available, it is probable that there is a lessening demand for application programmers. This means that at least some of the programmers are retrained into systems work for their later careers in an expanding IT.

Operations covers two main aspects — mainframe operators and data preparation operators. The former may also have limited career prospects with the levelling off of the numbers of mainframes. A similar problem arises as with programmers, i.e. how can they be retrained for other work? It does not necessarily follow that a high level of skill at mainframe operating makes a person suitable for retraining as a programmer or system analyst.

The continuing fluidity of the data processing scene has not yet allowed the careers of data processing staff to settle into formalised and qualification-based structures of other professions such as accountants.

Although Figure 9 illustrates a typical data processing department, in some companies the systems and programming sections may be merged under what may be termed systems development. Under a section manager, systems development would be found the combined post of programmer/analyst and the database administrator.

Here below is a brief description of the duties of the various kinds of data processing staff. Categorically stated are some five major duties of the top four in the department's hierarchy:

(i)   Data Processing Manager — In one organisation this person is in charge of systems work, programming and the day-to-day running of the computer. In another, he may merely be in charge of the operational aspects of data processing. Administrative ability is needed for either arrangement. His principal duties include:

(a) Participation in policy formulation.

(b) Assessing the effectiveness of the file maintenance procedures.

(c) Ensuring that program modifications are applied effectively.

(d) Ensuring that staff attend suitable training courses for their development.

(e) Assessing performance of staff for salary awards and promotion.

(ii)   Section Manager, Systems Analysis — As a designer and technical analyst, this person requires more technical knowledge than the business analyst. He is also sometimes a specialist in areas such as real-time systems, data capture, or data transmission. His principal duties include:

(a) Liaison with user departments to ensure that their requirements and problems are fully discussed before systems design and implementation.

(b) Comparing the cost and performance of alternative processing methods and techniques.

(c) Organising and reviewing systems documentation to ensure it complies with data processing standards.

(d) Reviewing the progress of projects and reporting status to the data processing manager.

(e) Presenting recommendations to data processing and user department management with regard to possible courses of action or design philosophy to achieve defined objectives.

(iii)   Section Manager, Programming — This person is usually an application programmer, who writes computer programs for use in business or scientific application. He also tests, documents and maintains application programs. An increasing proportion of applications programmers' time is spent on familiarising themselves and others with purchased application software. His principal duties, though, are:

(a) Liaison with the section manager, systems analysis to determine philosophy of proposed systems and establish the type of programming language to use — high-level or assembly code (low-level).

(b) Review of systems specification to establish the details of systems requirements before discussing these with assigned programmers.

(c) Defining test data requirements and monitoring test runs.

(d) Reviewing programmers' performance.

Jacob W. Chikuhwa

       (e) Reporting status of program development to the data processing manager.

(iv)   Section Manager, Operations — This is the most senior operator or administrator in charge of all operations. His principal duties include:

       (a) Development of operating schedules for all jobs to be run on the computer.

       (b) Ensuring that data is received on time from user departments.

       (c) Maintaining records on equipment utilisation.

       (d) Controlling stocks of data processing supplies, tapes, stationery and punched cards, etc.

       (e) Report to data processing manager of situations such as hardware malfunctions, staffing problems and other operational matters.

(v)   Business/Information Analyst — This post entails working with the end-user of a data processing system in order to define their information requirements. A good knowledge of business and manufacturing procedures is desirable as the business analyst is often the prime instigator of new systems.

(vi)   Programmer/Analyst — Does both of the systems analyst's and applications programmer's duties.

(vii)   Systems Programmer — This job differs from the applications programmer's in that a systems programmer designs and writes computer software programs such as operating systems, data managers, etc. This person is normally employed only by large user organisations, computer manufacturers or software houses.

(viii)   Database Administrator — This person controls the database, and as such is the sole adjudicator regarding modifications to the database's structure. He need not, however, be concerned with the actual contents of the database as this arises naturally from the activities of the user departments.

(ix)   Computer Operator — He operates the mainframe; this work mostly consisting of the loading and unloading of tape reels, disk cartridges, input media and output stationery; also concerned with maintaining contact with on-line and batch users. This is necessary in order to deal with contingencies such as erroneous source data and late results due to operational problems such as hardware breakdown and overloading of terminal facilities.

(x)   Data Processing Librarian/Data Controller — This is an administrative job in a larger data processing department. The data processing librarian logs work on and off the computer, and is in charge of the tape reels, disk cartridges, input media and documents before and after these have been through the computer room. This function may comprise two separate posts in some data processing departments.

(xi)   Data Entry/Preparation Clerk — This is a keypunch operator who transcribes source data into computer–sensible form.

(xii)   Ancillary Machine Operator — This person operates the stationery handling machines and may also be a computer operator or a data entry clerk at other times.

(xiii)   Management Service Manager — An organisation with a management services department is usually quite large and consequently its manager holds a fairly high-level post. Management services are normally taken to include data processing in all its aspects, O&M, OR and special services such as investment, insurance and legal matters.

Developments in the IT (Information Technology) field have shown that the structure and systems analysis continue to change dramatically.

APPENDIX

APPENDIX I

DATA COMPUTATION TECHNIQUES

Statistical Measurements
(i)   An average is a measure of central tendency and is the typical value in a group of data such as weekly or daily stock prices.
(ii)   An index number is a device for measuring the change that has taken place in a group of related items over a period of time, e. g. the price index.
(iii)   A correlation is the measurement of the degree of relationship between two or more separate sets of figures if there is a definite affinity between them. A correlation exists between petrol sales and the number of cars on the road.
(iv)   A time series is the measurement of changes that occur in a series of data over a period of time. A record of cars that were produced in each year from 1999 to 2010 is a time series.

Operational Research
    Operational research (OR) is the application of mathematical techniques to a wide variety of management problems. It was originally used to enhance military efficiency during the Second World War. In a corporation, OR is usually conducted by a team of accountants, engineers, statisticians, economists, scientists and mathematicians. The use of computers in OR is almost a necessity. In the OR process, a problem is defined and analysed, alternative solutions are tested and recommendation is made. Once the OR recommendation is placed into effect, it becomes a planning and controlling device.
    The OR techniques most often used by manufacturers are:
(i)   A computer simulation provides a method for observing the interaction of a number of important elements in a business problem. Various combinations of factors are studied in an attempt to see what will happen if some factors remain constant and others change. If these decisions were actually made one at a time, the possibility of expensive mistakes and the time required to note results would discourage making such experiments. By creating a model and by using a computer, the interaction of any

number of variables can be observed promptly and without any danger of losing money. For example, a manufacturing company can use a simulation model to experiment with alternative production scheduling processes.

(ii)   Linear programming is a mathematical device for determining the best way to allocate a limited amount of resources. In a linear programming problem all the relationships are expressed as linear or straight line, functions. That is if it takes four sales calls to make one sale, then it takes eight sales calls to make two sales. Since in most problems several linear functions are present, a computer generally is used to perform the complex calculations.

Linear programming can be used to resolve problems such as the assignment of salespersons and the location of facilities. For example, a problem of a company may be that its Mutare plants could not meet the market demand for tomato sauce while its Harare facilities produced more than the market required. With the help of linear programming, the firm can develop a freight schedule that economically matches the output of its six plants to the needs of its nearly seventy warehouses.

(iii)   Queuing theory is a mathematical technique for solving problems caused by waiting lines wherever they may occur. Queuing theory attempts to minimise expenditures by determining the proper balance between the cost of service and the cost of waiting line.

To illustrate, one company's problem was that at lunch time employees from several floors took the elevators to the company cafeteria. As a result, two waiting lines developed: one at the elevator and another in the cafeteria. A management consultant used queuing theory to solve this problem by designing a staggered lunch hour program for this company. Several other uses of queuing theory could be at a medical clinic where patients entering to receive medical attention may need a physician, nurse, clerical staff and related equipment and drugs; vehicle service station where vehicles driving into station for fuel and other services may need an attendant, petrol pump and other services.

Jacob W. Chikuhwa

Decision theory is the application of statistical probability theory in deciding the best policy to adopt to achieve an objective, e. g. a number of methods have various probabilities of success and lead to other tasks; which is the best set of methods to adopt in order to maximise success?

(iv)   Game theory is the application of statistical logic to competitive situations such as bidding for contracts.

(v)   Replacement theory is applied when deciding the best point of time to replace equipment subject to wear and tear in order to minimise the probability of sudden failure and also to minimise replacement costs.

(vi)   Inventory modelling determines the stock-holding levels and re-order quantities that give minimum overall stockholding costs. Taken into account are the separate costs such as capital invested, reordering and space occupied, and also the pattern of demand of the item.

(vii)   Assignment and allocation techniques are used for planning the optimum utilisation of resources, taking into consideration the characteristics of the resources and the requirements of the project, e.g. allocating skilled workers to tasks.

Depreciation

Depreciation is an annual charge against income that reflects the cost of the equipment used in the production process. In other words the purchase (cost) price of a machine must be charged against production during the machine's life; otherwise, profits will be overstated. To determine income, the annual charge is deducted from sales revenues, along with such other costs as labour and raw materials. However, depreciation is not a cash outlay. Funds were expended, say back in 2005, so the depreciation charged against income each year is not a cash outlay. In this way it differs from labour or raw materials payments.

There are four principal methods of depreciation, namely; straight line, sum-of-years digits, units of production and double declining balance.

Let us assume that a machine is purchased for $1 100 and has an estimated useful life of ten years or ten thousand hours. It will have a scrap value of $100 after ten years or ten thousand hours of use, whichever comes first.

Table 16 Comparison of Depreciation Methods for a 10-year, $1 100 Asset with a $100 Salvage Value

YEAR	STRAIGHT LINE ($)	SUM-OF-YEARS'-DIGITS ($)	UNITS OF PRODUCTION[2] ($)	DOUBLE DECLINING BALANCE ($)
1	100	182	200	220
2	100	164	180	176
3	100	145	150	141
4	100	127	130	113
5	100	109	100	90
6	100	91	80	72
7	100	73	60	58
8	100	55	50	46
9	100	36	30	42
10	100	18	20	42
TOTAL	**1 000**	**1 000**	**1 000**	**1 000**

(i)   Straight Line: With the straight line method, a uniform annual depreciation charge of $100 a year is provided. This figure is arrived at by simply dividing the economic life into the total cost of the machine minus the estimated salvage value:
($1 100 - $100 salvage value)/10 years = $100 a year depreciation charge.

---

[2] The assumption is made that the machine has used the following number of hours:
First year, 2 000; Second year, 1 800; Third year, 1 500; Fourth year, 1 300; Fifth year, 1 100;
Sixth year, 800; Seventh year, 600; Eighth year, 500; Ninth year, 300; Tenth year, 200.

Jacob W. Chikuhwa

If the estimated salvage value is not in excess of 10% of the original cost, it can be ignored, but we are leaving it in for illustrative purposes.

(ii)   Sum-of-Years'-Digits: Under the sum-of-years'–digits method, the yearly depreciation allowance is determined as follows:

(a) Calculate the sum-of-the-years' digits; in our example there is a total of 55 digits:

1+2+3+4+5+6+7+8+9+10 = 55. This figure can be arrived at by means of the sum of an algebraic progression equation where N is the life of the asset:

Sum = N (N+1)/2 = (10 (10+1)/2 = 55

(b) Divide the number of remaining years by the sum-of-years'–digits and multiply this fraction by the depreciation cost (total cost minus salvage value) of the asset:

Year 1: 10/55 ($1 000) = $182 depreciation charge
Year 2: 9/55 ($1 000) = $164 depreciation charge
....
....
....
Year 10: 1/55 ($1 000) = $18 depreciation charge

(iii)   Units of Production: Under the units of production method, the expected useful life of 10 000 hours is divided into the depreciable cost (purchase price minus salvage value) to arrive at an hourly depreciation rate of ten cents. Since in our example, the machine is run for 2 000 hours in the first year, the depreciation in that year is $200; in the second year $180; and so on. With this method, depreciation charges cannot be estimated precisely ahead of time; the firm must wait until the end of the year to determine what usage has been made of the machine and hence its depreciation.

(iv)   Double Declining Balance; The double declining balance method (DDB) is a special case of the declining balance method. The depreciation charge is calculated in DDB by multiplying a fixed rate times the cost less accumulated depreciation. Since the undepreciated balance becomes smaller in each successive period, the amount of depreciation declines during each successive period. The rate most commonly used is the maximum permitted for income tax purposes; usually twice the straight line method. Hence it is called the double decline balance method.

Table 17: Illustration of DDB Method

YEAR	Net Book Value $1000 Column 3 of Previous Year ($)	DDB Depreciation (0.20 x Column 2) ($)	Accumulated Depreciation (Sum of Column 3) ($)	Test of Straight Line Method ($)	Adjusted Accumulated Depreciation ($)
1	2	3	4	5	6
1	1 100	220	220		
2	880	176	396		
3	704	141	537		
4	563	113	650		
5	450	90	740		
6	360	72	812		
7	288	58	870		
8	230	46	916	43*	
9	184	37	953	42**	958
10	147	29	982	42	1 000

*$1 000 — $ 100 — $ 870 = $130 divided by 3 = $43

**$1 100 — $100 — $916 = 84 divided by 2 = $42

In DDB, the estimated salvage value is not usually subtracted from the cost of the asset in making the depreciation calculation, though that practice is followed in other depreciation methods. The DDB is illustrated for the data of our example;

Jacob W. Chikuhwa

Column 2 is the net book value subject to depreciation. It is the purchase price of the asset less the depreciation taken. For the second year the depreciation rate is applied to $1 000 less $220, or $880. The 20% of $880 is $176, the amount of depreciation for Year 2; and this procedure continues for each successive year.

The company makes a switch from DDB to straight line whenever straight line depreciation on the remaining amount under the DDB method. In the table above we test for this in the eighth year, but DDB depreciation is still somewhat higher.

In the ninth year, the depreciation amount of $1 000 less accumulated depreciation of 4916 equals $84, which is $42 per year for the remaining two years. The switch is made at this point so that the adjusted accumulated depreciation as shown in column 6 is the full $1 000 net depreciation value of the asset.

Thus, although the salvage value is not initially taken into account in applying the DDB method, it is not ignored. The method we have illustrated is used when the salvage value is relatively small. Strictly applied, the salvage value has a substantial impact on the depreciation rate applied. The formula for computing the rate under the declining balance method when the salvage value is relatively large is:

Depreciation Rate $= I - Z/ I^{1/N}$ where

N = Estimated periods of service life

Z = Estimated salvage value

I = Purchase price of the asset.

Thus, for $N = 8$ years, $Z = \$2\ 000$, and $I = \$12\ 000$, we have

Depreciation Rate $= I\ (2\ 000/12\ 000)^{1/8}$

$$= I - 0{,}80 = 0{,}20 = 20\%$$

If N is changed to 4 years, we have

Depreciation Rate $= I - (2\ 000/12\ 000)^{1/4}$

$$I - 0{,}64 = 0{,}36 = 36\%$$

Thus, although the depreciation rate under the declining balance method is applied to the full investment cost before the estimated salvage value is deducted, the amount of the depreciation and its time pattern under that declining balance are affected by the amount of the estimated salvage value.

Effect of Depreciation on Taxes Paid. The effect of the accelerated methods on a firm's income tax payment is easily demonstrated. If a firm chooses in the first year to use the straight line method, it can deduct only $100 from its earnings to arrive at earnings before taxes (the amount of earnings to which the tax rate applies). However, using any one of the other three methods, the firm would have a much greater deduction and, therefore, a lower tax liability. When tax laws are changed to permit more rapid, or accelerated depreciation, this reduces tax payments and stimulates business investments.

The sum-of-years'–digits and the double decline balance methods are generally referred to as accelerated depreciation methods; ordinarily, they are more favourable than straight line depreciation from a tax point of view.

The fiscal implications of depreciation methods stem from two factors:

(i)   Accelerated depreciation reduces taxes in the early years of an asset's life, thus increasing corporate cash flows and making more funds available for investment and

(ii)   Faster cash flows increase the profitability, or rate of return, on an investment.

Financial Forecasting

Percent of Sales Method

The most important variable that influences a firm's financing requirements is its projected dollar volume of sales. A good sales forecast is an essential foundation for forecasting financial requirements.

The simplest approach to forecasting financial requirements expresses the firm's needs in terms of the percentage of annual sales invested in each individual balance sheet item. As an example, consider the balance sheet in Table 18. The firm's sales are running at about $500000 a year, which is its capacity limit; the profit margin after tax on sales is 4 percent. During 2005, the firm earned $20 000 after taxes and paid out $10 000 in dividends. How much additional financing will be needed if

Jacob W. Chikuhwa

sales expand to $80 000 during 2006? The calculating procedure, using the percent of sales method, is as follows:[3]

First, isolate those balance sheet items that can be expected to vary directly with sales. In the case of a firm represented by Table 18, this step applies to each category of assets, a higher level of sales necessitates more cash for transactions, more receivables, higher inventory levels and additional fixed plant capacity. On the liability side, accounts payable as well as accruals may be expected to increase as sales do. Retained earnings will go up as long as the firm is profitable and does not pay out 100 percent of earnings, but the percentage increase is not constant. However, neither common stock nor mortgage bonds will increase spontaneously with an increase in sales.

Table 18: Balance Sheet as of December 31, 2005 ($)

ASSETS			LIABILITIES
Cash	10 000	Accounts Payable	50 000
Receivables	85 000	Accrued Taxes and Wages	25 000
Inventories	100 000	Mortgage Bonds	70 000
Fixed Assets (net)	150 000	Common Stocks	100 000
		Retained Earnings	100 000
		TOTAL LIABILITIES AND	
TOTAL ASSETS	**345 000**	**NET WORTH**	**345 000**

[3] We should recognise, of course, that as a practical matter, business firms plan their needs in terms of specific items of equipment, square meters of floor space and other factors, and not as a percentage of sales. However, the outside analyst does not have access to this information; even though the information on specific items is available, a manager needs to check forecasts in aggregate terms. The percent of sales method serves both these needs surprisingly well.

Table 19: Balance Sheet as
of December 31, 2005 (%)

ASSETS   LIABILITIES

Cash	2,0	Accounts Payable	10,0
Receivables	17,0	Accrued Taxes and Wages	5,0
Inventories	20,0	Mortgage Bonds*	
Fixed Assets (net)	30,0	Common Stocks*	
		Retained Earnings	
		TOTAL LIABILITIES AND	
TOTAL ASSETS	**69,0**	**NET WORTH**	**15,0**

Assets as Percent of Sales
Less: Spontaneous Increase in Liabilities
Percent of each additional dollar of sales that must be financed
*Not applicable

The items that can be expected to vary directly with sales are
tabulated as a percentage of sales in Table 19. For every $1,00 increase
in sales, assets must increase $0,69; this $0,69 must be financed in some
manner. Accounts payable will increase spontaneously with sales, as
will accruals; these two items will supply $0,15 of new funds for each
$1,00 increase in sales. Subtracting 15% for spontaneously generated
funds from the 69% funds requirement leaves 54%. Thus, for each $1,00
increase in sales, the firm must obtain $0,54 of financing either from
internally generated funds or from external sources.

In the case at hand, sales are scheduled to increase from $500 000 to
$800 000 or by $30 000. Applying the 54% developed in the table to the
expected increase in sales will lead to the conclusion that $162 000 will
be needed.

Some of that need will be met by retained earnings. Total revenues
during 2006 will be $800000; if the firm earns 4% after taxes on this
volume, profits will amount to $32 000. Assuming that the 50%
dividend payout ratio is maintained, dividends will be $16 000 and $16
000 will be retained. Subtracting the retained earnings from the

Jacob W. Chikuhwa

$162 000 that was needed leaves a figure of $146 000, the amount of funds that must be obtained through borrowing or by selling new common stock.

This process may be expressed in equation form:

EXTERNAL FUNDS NEEDED = A/TR (ΔTR) – B/TR (ΔTR) - bm (TR$_2$)..........(1)

Here

A/TR = Assets that increase spontaneously with total revenues or sales as a percent of total revenues or sales.

B/TR = Those liabilities that increase spontaneously with total revenues or sales as a percent of total revenues or sales.

ΔTR = Change in total revenues or sales.

m = Profit margin on sales

TR$_2$ = Total revenues projected for the year.

b = Earnings retention ratio.

For figures in Tables 18 and 19 then,

EXTERNAL FUNDS NEEDED = 0.69 ($300 000) – 0.15 ($300 000) – 0.5 (0,04) ($800 000)

$$= 0.54\ (\$300\ 000) - 0.02\ (\$800\ 000)$$
$$= \$146\ 000.$$

The $146 000 found by the formula method must, of course, equal the amount derived previously.

Notice what would have occurred if the firm's sales forecast for 2006 had been only $515000 or a 3% increase. Applying the formula, we find the external funds requirements as follows:

EXTERNAL FUNDS NEEDED = 0.54 ($15 000) – 0.02 ($515 000)

$$= \$8\ 100 - \$10\ 300$$
$$= (\$2\ 200)$$

In this case, no external funds are required. In fact, the firm will have $2 200 in excess of its requirements; it should therefore plan to increase dividends, retire debt, or seek additional investment opportunities. The example shows that while small percentage increases in sales can be financed through internally generated funds, larger percentage increases cause the firm to go into the market for outside capital. In other words, small rates of sales growth can be financed from external sources, but higher rates of sales growth require external financing. At this point in time, one might ask two questions:

"Shouldn't depreciation be considered as a source of funds, and won't this reduce the amount of external funds needed?" The answer to both questions is no. In the percent of sales method, we are relating fixed assets, net of the reserve for depreciation, to sales. This process implicitly assumes that funds related to the depreciation policies are used to replace assets to which the depreciation is applicable. The net fixed assets related to sales already have the reserve for depreciation (which is a cumulative sum of each year's depreciation change) deducted from gross fixed assets.

It is necessary to note that the sales level equals $(1 + g)$ TR_1 , where g = the growth rate in sales. The increase in sales can therefore, be written:

$$\Delta TR = (1 + g)\ TR_1 - TR = TR_1\ (1 + g - 1)\ = gTR_1$$

Let us next take the expression for external funds needed, Equation (1) and use it to derive the percentage of the increase in sales that will have to be financed externally (percentage of external funds required, or PEFR) as a function of the critical variables involved.

In Equation (1) let $(A/TR\ B/TR) = I$
Substitute for ΔTR and TR_2 and divide both sides by ΔTR - gTR = gTR_1,

$$PEFR\ = I - m/g\ (1 + g)\ b \dots\dots\dots\dots\dots\dots\ (2)$$

Using Equation (2), we can now investigate the influence of factors such as an increased rate of inflation on the percentage of sales growth that must be financed externally. Based on relationships for all manufacturing industries, some representative values of the terms on the right hand side of the equation are:

$$I = 0.5,\ m\ = 0.05,\ and\ b\ = 0.60$$

During the period that preceded the onset of inflation in the Western economies after 1966, the economy was growing at about 6 to 7 percent per annum. If a firm was in an industry that grew at the same rate as the economy as a whole and if a firm maintained its market share position in

Jacob W. Chikuhwa

its industry, the firm grew at six to seven percent per annum as well. Let us see what the implication for external financing requirements would be. With the growth rate of 6% the percentage of an increase in sales that would have to be financed externally would be as follows:

$$PEFR = 0.5 - 0.05/0.06\ (1.06)\ (0.6)$$
$$= 0.50 - 0.53 = -0.03\ = -3\%$$

At 7% growth, the PEFR would be:

$$PEFR = 0.5 - 0.05/0.07\ (1.07)\ (0.7)$$
$$= 0.50 - 0.46 = 0.04\ = 4\%$$

Thus, at a growth rate of 6% the percentage of external financing to sales growth would be a negative 3%. In other words, the firm would have excess funds which it could use to increase dividends or increase its investment in marketable securities. With a growth rate of 7%, the firm would have a requirement of external financing of 4% of the sales increase.

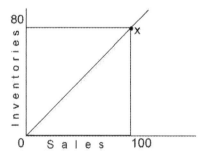

Fig. 10: Percent of Sales

The percent of sales method of financial forecasting assumes that certain balance sheet items vary directly with sales; i.e. that the ratio of a given balance sheet item to sales remains constant. The postulated relationship is shown in Fig. 10. Note that the percent of sales method implicitly assumes a linear relationship that passes through the origin. The slope of the line representing the relationship may vary, but the line always passes through the origin. Implicitly, the relationship is established by finding one point, or ratio, such as that designated as x in

Fig. 10 and then connecting this point with the origin. Then, for any projected level of sales, the forecasted level of the particular balance sheet item can be determined.

Experience in applying the technique of percent of sales in practice suggests the importance of understanding;

(i)   the basic technology of the firm
(ii)   the logic of the relation between sales and assets for the particular firm in question.

A great deal of experience and judgement is required to apply the technique in actual practice.

The percent of sales method is most appropriately used for forecasting relatively short term changes in financing needs. It is less useful for longer term forecasting for reasons best described in connection with the regression method of financial forecasting.

Scatter Diagram or Simple Regression Method

An alternative method used for forecasting financial requirements is the scatter diagram, or simple regression method. A scatter diagram is a graphic portrayal of joint relations. The data is displayed as a collection of points, each having the value of one variable determining the position on the horizontal axis and the value of the other variable determining the position on the vertical axis.

If a parameter exists that is systematically incremented and/or decremented by the other, it is called the *control parameter* or independent variable and is customarily plotted along the horizontal axis. The measured or dependent variable is customarily plotted along the vertical axis. If no dependent variable exists, either type of variable can be plotted on both axis and a scatter plot will illustrate only the degree of correlation (not causation) between two variables.

A scatter plot can suggest various kinds of correlations between variables with a certain confidence interval. Correlations may be positive (rising), negative (falling), or null (uncorrelated). If the pattern of dots slopes from lower left to upper right, it suggests a positive correlation between the variables being studied (Fig. 11). If the pattern of dots slopes from upper left to lower right, it suggests a negative correlation. A line of best fit (alternatively called 'trendline') can be drawn in order to study the correlation between the variables.

Jacob W. Chikuhwa

Proper use of the scatter diagram method requires practical, but not necessarily statistical sophistication.

Table 20 presents data on sales and investments for a firm for the ten year 1997 to 2006 period. The data are graphed in Fig. 11. Using a hand calculator, the line of best fit for the points, or the regression line, was calculated to be:

Inventories = $216 million plus 0.05 sales.

Table 20: Inventory to Sales Relationship for 1997 to 2006 ($ million)

YEAR	INVENTORY (Y)	SALES (X)	INVENTORY TO SALES RATIO (Y/X)
1997	403	4 560	0,088
1998	461	4 962	0,093
1999	506	5 728	0,088
2000	507	6 477	0,078
2001	665	8 480	0,078
2002	1 087	17 924	0,061
2003	1 165	17 524	0,066
2004	1 278	20 181	0,063
2005	1 438	21 752	0,066
2006	1 216	24 106	0,050

This regression line was then drawn in on Fig. 11.

As can be seen, the points are all relatively close to the calculated regression line. The correlation coefficient between sales and inventories for these data is 0.9745, indicating only a relatively small scatter of the actual data off the regression line.

Appendix

The relationship appears to be a straight line. A number of offsetting influences seem to be operating. Inventories increase as the square root of sales. The line would be curved downwards somewhat. Also, the greater efficiencies in handling inventories such as improved transportation would also tend to cause the percentage of inventories to sales to decrease over time as sales increase. But the greater variety of products would cause inventories to rise as sales volume and product diversity increases. These influences appear to be counterbalancing, since the actual data in the table indicate that the straight line calculated is a very good fit to the data.

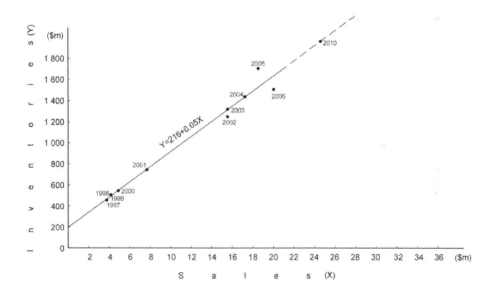

Fig. 11 Inventory to Sales Relationships (1997 - 2006)

Suppose that a sales forecast has been made for 2010 for a firm as represented by the table which projects that sales will increase at the same rate as between 2002 and 2006, a period when they increased by about 35%. This would result in sales of $32 543m for 2010. Given all of the uncertainties of the economic market, a sales forecast for 2010 would require a very comprehensive study. But our interest is in developing the relations between sales and inventories. Taking the sales

Jacob W. Chikuhwa

forecast as given, what projection for inventories would be appropriate? Table 20 shows that the ratio of inventories to sales has been in a downward trend for the firm, from over 9% in 1998 to 5% in 2006. But this result is mainly due to a mathematical relationship resulting from the positive amount of inventory as the intercept of the regression line. For example, consider the inventory to sales relationships for inventories forecast from the use of the regression line for the following levels in Table 21 (in millions of dollars).

As sales rise, the ratio of inventories to sales declines from 0.0932 to 0.0572. Use of the ratio of 0.0932 based on sales level $5 000m would have resulted in a forecast of inventories related to $30 000m sales of $2 796m instead of $1 716m.; an upside error of $1 080m. This is due to the mathematical influence of the base stock inventory $216m in the regression equation. This constant has a greater influence when sales are small than when sales are large.

Table 21: Inventory to Sales Relationships for Inventories Forecast

SALES	INVENTORIES	RATIO OF INVENTORIES TO SALES
5 000	466	0.0932
10 000	716	0.0716
20 000	1 216	0.0608
30 000	1 716	0.0572

Note: These data are based on the use of the regression equation:

Inventories = $216m + 0.05 sales.

Thus, if we had a sales forecast of sales for 2010 in the case of the firm (as in Table 20) of $32 543m, the forecast of inventories, using the regression line, would be $1 843m. Using the ratio of inventories to sales, we might use the average ratio of 0,0612 for 2002 – 2006 to get an inventory projection of $1 992m, which is greater by $149m than the forecast using the regression method. If we used the low ratio for 2006, which was 5% we would be $216m lower than with the projection by use of the regression method.

The percentage of sales method of projecting financing requirements will be unstable if the regression line for the data does not go through the origin. The regression method is thus seen to be superior to the percentage of sales method of forecasting financial requirements. When a firm is likely to have a base stock inventory of fixed assets, the ratio of that item to sales declines as sales increase. In such a case, using historical relations between inventory and sales, for example, would set too high a norm, or control standard, as compared with the use of the regression method. This is an important difference between the two forecasting methods.

The scatter diagram method differs from the percent of sales method principally in that it does not assume that the line of relationship passes through the origin. In its simplest form, the scatter diagram method calls for calculating the ratio between sales and the relevant balance sheet item at two points in time, extending a line through these two points, and using the line to describe the relationship between sales and the balance sheet item. The accuracy of the regression is improved if more points are plotted, and the regression line can be fitted mathematically (by a technique known as the method of least squares) as well as drawn in by eye.

In Figure 12, the scatter diagram is compared to the percent-of-sales forecast. The error induced by the use of the percent-of- sales method is represented by the gap between the two lines. At the sales level of 125, the percent of sales method would call for an inventory of 100 versus an inventory of only 90 using a scatter diagram forecast. Note that the error is very small if sales continue to run at approximately the current level, but the gap widens and the error increases as sales deviate in either direction from current levels, as they probably would if a long-run forecast were being made.

Linear scatter diagram, or linear regression, assumes that the slope of the regression line is constant. Although this condition does frequently exist, it is not a universal rule. Fig. 13 illustrates the application of curvilinear simple regression to forecasting financial relationships. We

Jacob W. Chikuhwa

have drawn this hypothetical illustration to show a flattering curve, which implies a decreasing relationship between sales and inventory beyond point X, the current level of operations. In this case, the forecast of inventory requirements at a sales level of 125 would be too high if the linear regression method was used (but too low if sales declined from 100 to 50).

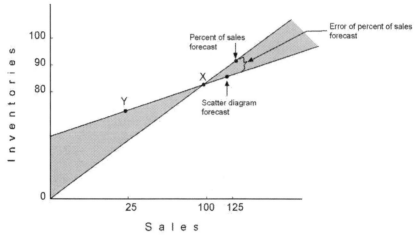

Fig. 12: Scatter Diagram or Simple Linear Regression

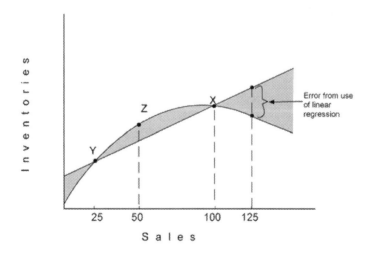

Fig. 13 Curvilinear Simple Regression

Appendix

Multiple Regression Analysis

In the illustrations to this point, it has been assumed that the observations fell exactly on the relationship line. This implies perfect correlation, something that, in fact, seldom occurs. In practice, the actual observations would be scattered about the regression line as shown in Fig. 14. What causes the deviations from regression line? One answer, if linear regression is used, is that the actual line of relationship might be curvilinear. But if curvilinear regression is used and deviation still occurs, we must seek other explanations for the scatter around the regression line. The most obvious answer is that inventories are determined by factors in addition to sales.

Fig. 14 Deviations in the Forecast

A more sophisticated approach to forecasting a firm's assets calls for the use of multiple regression analysis. In simple regression, sales are assumed to be a function of only one variable; in multiple regression, sales are recognised to depend upon a number of variables. For example, in simple regression, we might state that sales are strictly a function of GNP. With multiple regression, we might state that sales depend on both GNP and a set of additional variables. For example, sales of tennis equipment depend upon:

(i) the general level of prosperity as measured by GNP, personal disposable income, or other indicators of aggregate economic activity;

Jacob W. Chikuhwa

    (ii) population increases;
    (iii) number of tennis courts built;
    (iv) advertising, etc.

In the illustration above, inventory levels are certainly influenced by work stoppages at the plants of suppliers. A department store owner anticipating a strike in the cooking oil manufacturing industry will stock up on cooking oil. Such hedge buying would cause actual inventories to be above the level forecast on the basis of sales projections. Then, assuming a strike does occur and continues for many months, inventories will be drawn down and may end up well below the predicted level. Multiple regression techniques, which introduce additional variables (such as work stoppages) into the analysis, are employed to further improve financial forecasting.

The need to employ more complicated forecasting techniques varies from situation to situation. For example, the percent of sales method may be perfectly adequate for making short term forecasts where conditions are relatively stable, while curvilinear or multiple regression may be deemed essential for longer term forecasts in more dynamic industries. As in all other applications of financial analysis, the cost of using more refined techniques must be balanced against the benefits of increased accuracy. Most computer installations now have canned regression programs incorporated into their systems, making it extremely easy to use multiple regression techniques. At least in the large corporation, multiple regression is widely used.

<u>Inflation and Its Measurement</u>

In an effort to measure inflation, it is necessary to consider the following factors:

(i)   To monitor the state of balance between the supply of goods and services and demand for them, it is necessary to review the movement of prices and costs against the background of information relating to production and incomes. Current appraisals will generally have to lean heavily on the analysis of *price trends*. This may be supplemented by a parallel analysis of changes in the *supply of money*.

(ii)   Where imports are large in relation to production for domestic use, *market prices* are strongly influenced from abroad and thus tend to be poorer indicators of internal balance, particularly in the smaller developing countries. Where *government revenue* is raised largely by *indirect taxation*, changes in prices may reflect changes in taxes as well as relative movement of demand or supply.

(iii) Storage and stock inadequacies tend to give rise to wide *seasonal fluctuations* and in some places even the arrival (or tardiness) of a cargo ship from abroad can make a significant difference to local prices.

(iv) The less developed the economy and the greater the weight of imports among marketed goods, the less relevant are local prices as indicators of internal balance. This is particularly true in the case of prices at the wholesale level whose usefulness in the present context depends very largely on the extent of domestic production of the goods concerned. The limited degree of industrialisation often results in a *price index* that is not really representative of the situation among domestic producers.

It is due to the numerous numbers of factors that there is no precise mathematical formula for calculating inflation. Basically, it is a situation in which prices are rising and pressures exist to accentuate the fall in the value of money. If, for example, incomes increase and this increase in the volume of money available for exchange transactions is not required by or followed by an appropriate expansion in the number of transactions then a situation exists in which prices will tend to rise. Should income spending fall (or hoarding increases) and the number of exchange transactions fall even more, then a similar tendency exists.

An increase in income spending is sometimes called the "demand-pull"; it may arise if the quantity of money in circulation is expanded. A similar effect would result if money circulated more quickly as a result of more purchases, i.e. an increase in the velocity of circulation.

This may be called "demand inflation" for, as effective demand increases (whether because of higher wages — the "wages-pull" — easier financial conditions or other reasons) output and employment are pushed up. If the capacity of the economy is underutilised and there is unemployment, there is no problem. But, if the general increase in activity means an increase in the demand for a limited supply of the

Jacob W. Chikuhwa

factors, e.g. raw materials, then shortages develop, labour difficulties tend to arise, a "cost-push" develops and the prices of products rises.

It is accepted that the monetary authorities are duty bound to attempt to control inflation should it threaten the stability of the currency, either internally or externally. There are serious inconveniences in using money that fluctuates in value; if a reasonable measure of stability is not preserved the whole basis on which economic activity rests is threatened. Expenditure and income are measured in monetary units and with unstable units the planning of future activity becomes difficult and adds to existing uncertainties.

APPENDIX II

ORGANISATION CHARTS

Fig. 15: Human Resources Department

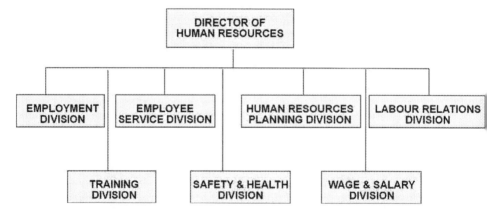

The establishment of functional departments within a company arises from the need for specialisation. As a business concern expands, there arises the necessity to adapt to a complex, changing environment. Figures 15 to 18 reflect a marked degree of specialisation.

Fig. 15 shows the Human Resources Department, also known as the Personnel Department. The Director reports to the Director General,

Appendix

who is the Chief Executive. Under the Director may be a diverse number of branches (units) of which Employment Service (Employee Welfare) Division and Labour Relations (Industrial Relations) Division took quite a central position during the late 1980s.

Fig. 16 shows the tradition accounts department with the Chief Accountant at the head. It is pertinent to note that the rapid growth of computer-based financial data processing has radically affected the structure of both the Accounts and Finance departments. There is an inclination towards the creation of such a department as would cater for the functions of economics and statistics, i.e. an Economics and Statistics Department (Fig. 18). Traditionally, data processing originated in the accounting area, since most record keeping was done there. However, the increasingly important statistics discipline has had a big impact on both the accounts and finance branches of specialisation. The result has been a trend leading to the merger of accounts and finance functions into an "Econo-Stats" Department. In our example, the Manager would report to the General Manager who is the Chief Executive in this case.

Fig. 16: Accounting Department

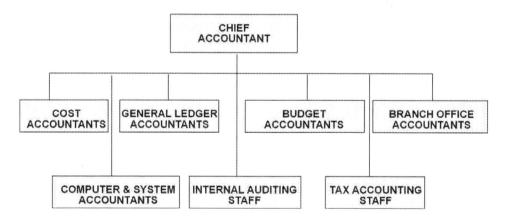

Jacob W. Chikuhwa

Fig. 17: Finance Department

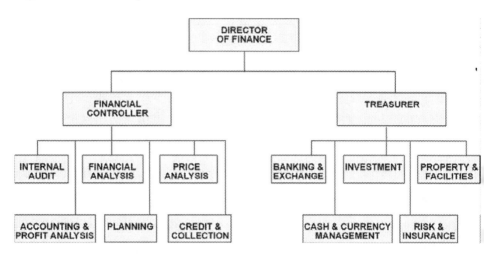

Management has recognised that information is a scarce and valuable resource of the entire organisation and has increasingly emphasised the statistical data-processing activity and elevated it in the organisational structure. While economists and statisticians play a dominant role in the department, its functions are now biased towards computer-base accounting and financial applications.

Therefore, the creation of an econo-stats department should be accompanied by the elevation of its activity to the same status as the tradition line functions (production, marketing, finance, personnel). When it occupies this position, the department reflects a corporate-wide scope. The department's name should be associated with management information systems (MIS) and could be renamed MIS Department. The independent status of the "Econo-Stats" Department helps to ensure that each functional area gets impartial service and that their particular information requirements are integrated to meet organisation goals.

Fig. 18: Economics and Statistics

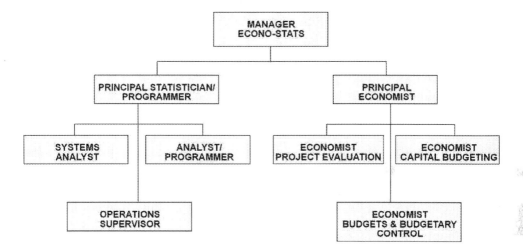

Jacob W. Chikuhwa

Fig. 19: Overall View of the Total Budgeting Process

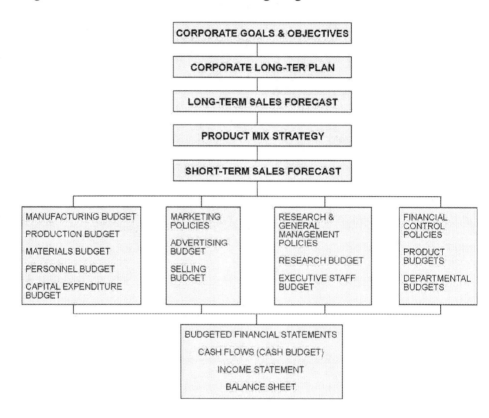

GLOSSARY

AAAA

account: In book-keeping an account is a ledger record of debits and credits. On the Stock Exchange the term refers to the period of time in which dealings are done on a credit basis.

accounting: Art of preparing reports from book-keeping records, based on accounting concepts and measurement conventions.

accounting concepts: Accounting principles. Practical rules which enable book-keeping records of transactions to be converted into accounting reports.

accounting period: Period of time from one balance sheet to the next. Period of the profit and loss account.

accounting reports: Balance sheet, profit and loss account and cash flow forecasts.

account payable: Creditor. Money owed by a business. Current liability.

account receivable: Debtor. Money owed to the business.

accruals: Liability. Creditor. Payable. Current liability. Accounting concept: Income and expenditure for the accounting period must be included whether for cash or credit.

accrued interest: Interest on securities, etc., which has accumulated but which has not been paid or collected.

accumulated profit: Retained earnings. Balance of profit retained in business.

administrative expense: Cost of directing and controlling business. Includes directors fees, office salaries, office rent, lighting, heating, legal fees, auditors fees, accounting services, etc. Not research, manufacturing, sales or distribution expenses.

application program: A computer program designed to solve a particular type of problem or perform a specific operation.

appropriation: This is the act of setting money aside before formally authorising the spending of it.

arithmetic mean: The familiar average obtained by dividing the total of all values by the number of values. A weighted arithmetic mean takes account of the fact that in some collections of numbers some of them are more important than others. (See central tendency.)

Jacob W. Chikuhwa

asset: Something owned by the business which has a measurable cost. (See current, earning, fixed, floating, intangible and wasting assets.)

assignment and allocation techniques: Used for planning the optimum utilisation of resources, taking into consideration the characteristics of the resources and requirements of the profit, e.g. allocating skills workers to tasks.

audit: Official examination of accounts. Audit can be internal or external. An internal audit is performed by a unit (department) within a given firm and an external audit is performed by an independent firm of auditors (consultants).

authorised capital: Share capital of the business authorised by law. May be only partly issued for cash. Ordinary of preference shares.

average: A measure of central tendency; a typical value in a group of data such as weekly wages or student ages in a class.

BBBB

bad debt: Debtor who fails to pay. Amount written off to expense.

balance: Difference between the debits and credits in a ledger account.

balance sheet: Accounting report. Statement of assets owned by a business and the way they are financed from liabilities and owner's equity. Does not indicate the market value of the business.

bank: A firm, usually a joint-stock company, formed to perform one or more of the following functions: provide a safe place for the deposit of cash or valuables; advance money; issue notes; facilitate payments by book-entries; discount commercial bills; and act as an agent in a variety of other ways.

batch processing: A method of processing data in which transactions are accumulated for a predetermined period of time and prepared in batches for computer input as a single unit.

binary system: The numeric system used in computer operations that uses the digits 0 and 1 has a base of 2.

blocked account: When foreign holders of a country's currency, or assets expressed in terms of that currency, cannot freely use such holdings, they are said to be 'blocked'.

bond: A document, by signing which an obligation is made to pay a specified sum in the future. It is a certificate of indebtedness, and is classed with annuities and debentures as debts owed by a government, public body or company.

book-keeping: Recording of transactions in debits and credits. Posting of transactions from journals to ledgers to provide data for accounting reports.

book value: (a) Value of assets in the books. (b) Value of ordinary shares in the books. (Computed: Owner's equity less preference shares, divided by the number of ordinary shares.)

break-even point: That point in production at which total costs equal total revenue, where no abnormal profit is received.

budget: Annual estimate of revenue and expenditure of a business or country. Private person's or family's similar estimate. Amount of money needed or available for the business. It is a part of a broader financial planning and control process.

buildings: Fixed assets unless acquired for resale. Depreciated to expenses over their working life. Balance sheet value and cost less depreciation. Not market value. Sometimes re-valued periodically. Land is not depreciated.

building society: A building society provides long-term loans on the security of property (see mortgage) for the purchase of houses for owner-occupation. Funds are obtained from the general public, who are paid a rate of interest lower than that charged to borrowers.

business: Habitual occupation, profession, trade carried out with the objective to make a profit or living.

business as a system: A combination of related functional groups (departments) headed by a Chief Executive, supported by a group of departmental heads. For example, the production department is a functional group or a subsystem within the environment of a total system (the business) consisting of integrated physical and control systems.

business cycle: Also known as trade cycle, it is a general fluctuation in the economic activity of a society, where the means of production are mainly privately owned. The fluctuation is from a period of prosperity, or boom, down, through a recession, to depression, or slump, then a recovery to prosperity through a period known as revival. These fluctuations are characterised by expansions and contractions in most

Jacob W. Chikuhwa

aspects of economic life, namely employment and unemployment, industrial production, earning and spending of wages and other incomes, the buying and selling of securities, domestic and foreign trade, and prices.

business studies: Training in economics, management, marketing, etc.

business synergies: Synergy, in general, may be defined as two or more things functioning together to produce a result not independently obtainable. That is, if elements A and B are combined, the result is greater than the expected arithmetic sum A+B.

business systems: A combination of related subsystems consisting of a series of operations arranged in a logical sequence to achieve a particular purpose as efficiently as possible, e.g. payroll system, stock control system, accounts payable, accounts receivable, etc.

buyers' market: A condition in a market when prices are low, i.e. favourable to buyers. This usually means that there is an excess of supply over demand and sellers are willing to accept lower prices to dispose of their goods or services.

CCCC

capital: The central theme of modern definitions is that capital is a "produced means of production" or "wealth set aside for the production of further wealth". Capital may be in the form of money or goods; this is accumulated from the proceeds of past production and is used to acquire, by a process called investment, capital goods, which will be used in conjunction with other factors to produce goods of a capital or consumer nature, or services. The following is a selection of different types of capital: (a) Authorised or nominal capital: the amount of share capital fixed by a company's Memorandum of Association. (b) Circulating capital: either that which fulfils its function in one use, i.e. which is completely consumed and merged into a new product or that which must be transformed physically to be productive. (c) Fixed capital: that which is in durable form and can be used repeatedly; may include goodwill, i.e. intangible fixed capital. (d) Loan capital: see debenture. (e) Paid-up capital: the amount of authorised capital that has been subscribed. (f) Personal capital: the personal skill possessed by a person as a result of training. (g) Producer's, trade or real capital: raw materials and plant used directly for production. (h) Share capital: the capital issued by companies in the form of securities. (i) Working capital: synonymous with floating capital, i.e. capital which can perform more than one function, e.g. money.

capital expenditure: The amount paid to acquire an asset. (See investment.)

capital gains tax: A tax that is paid upon the profit made for the buying and selling of assets.

capital market: A network of institutions through which the savings and surplus funds of the economy are channelled to commerce and industry, local and central government, both domestic and foreign. A capital market consists of the savers, the borrowers and the intermediaries.

cash: Money asset of a business. Includes both cash in hand and cash at bank. Balance sheet current asset. For an individual, cash would be actual coins and bank notes in his possession; he may regard his current bank account as cash although the cheque is not legal tender. A bank regards notes and coins in till and vaults and its balances at the Central (Reserve) Bank as cash. In certain circumstances, however, the monetary authorities may prevent a bank from freely drawing upon such a balance.

cash flow: The pattern and extent of cash payments and receipts by a business over a particular period. Also used to describe the difference between total cash inflow and total cash outflow for a specific project.

cash transactions: Receipt or payment of cash.

centralised data processing: A concept where an organisation has all its computing equipment located at the same site while field office operations have no effective data processing capability.

central processing unit: The component of a computer system with the computing equipment located at the same site while field office operations have no effective data processing capability control element, arithmetic/logic element and primary storage element to control the interpretation and execution of instructions. It does not include input and output elements nor secondary on-line storage.

central tendency: A measure of this, namely an average, is a single numerical statement of the general magnitude of all the values in a

Jacob W. Chikuhwa

distribution. It reflects the tendency of the data to concentrate at certain central values.

change file: A temporary data file containing changes to be made in the records of a master file during a particular processing cycle.

cheque: A written order to a banker to pay the person bearing it, or a person or body named on it, a specified sum of money. A cheque is not legal tender and a creditor can, therefore, refuse payment by one. If the cheque is "open", i.e. does not have two lines drawn parallel across its face, the banker will cash to the person presenting the cheque. If the cheque is "crossed" with the two lines mentioned above, then the appropriate amount will be paid into the person's account, i.e. the payment will be effected by book-entries. The legal definition of a cheque is "a bill of exchange drawn on a banker payable on demand".

CIF: A contract in which the payment for the goods includes the cost of insurance and freight.

claims: Claims against the assets of business. Owners or creditors. Total claims equal total assets. Creditors' claims are called liabilities. Owners claims are called owners' equity.

closed shop: A business in which only members of a trade union will be accepted for employment.

COBOL: (Common Business-Oriented Language) A high-level programming language generally used for accounting and business data processing.

coefficient: An expression of a mathematical relationship. Significant coefficients in economics are those relating to the accelerator and elasticity of supply and demand.

collateral security: Property, perhaps in the form of deeds to a house or stocks and shares, deposited with a creditor to guarantee that a loan will be repaid.

collective bargaining: The existence of trade union and employers' associations makes it easier for both sides in a dispute to meet and bargain for changes in wages, hours of work, working conditions, etc. Thus, the bargaining is done collectively, by representatives of both sides.

company: Legal entity. Limited or unlimited. Regulated by the Companies Act. May be either private or public, i.e. may be either a private limited company or a public joint-stock company. The former may have between two and fifty shareholders; the latter from seven upwards, with no maximum.

competition: A market condition in which there is an indeterminate number of buyers and sellers, each intent on maximising profit or satisfaction and in which price is subject to control only by the forces of supply and demand. This condition, in which no single trade can exert influence, is sometimes called free competition, and approximates to perfect competition.

computer: Calculator, reckoner. A mechanical moron which can handle only quantifiable data. An automatic electronic apparatus for making calculations or controlling operations that are expressible in numerical or logical terms.

computer program: A series of instructions or statements prepared in a form acceptable to a computer that will yield a planned result.

computer simulation: The use of a computer in observing the interaction of a number of important elements in a business problem. Various combinations of factors are studied in an attempt to see what will happen if some factors remain constant and others change.

conciliation: The act of bringing two parties together in an attempt to find a peaceful way out of a difficulty. In the case of a dispute between employers and employees it is the interest of the public and the disputants themselves that all possible methods of reaching a settlement should be tried, if, for example, a strike or lock-out has been threatened.

consumer: The person for whom consumer goods have utility, i.e. have the ability to satisfy a want.

consumer good: Something used for direct satisfaction of human wants; it may be short- or long-lived. The expression is used to distinguish those goods which are not capital goods.

co-operatives: A legal business structure, where the members who own the business must also work in the business. Each member has one vote. Co-operative societies may be divided, broadly, into two categories: consumers and producers.

correlation: The measurement of the degree of relationship between two or more separate sets of figures if there is a definite affinity between them.

Jacob W. Chikuhwa

cost: (a) Expenditure on a given thing (article). (b) To compute the cost of something. (c) Direct or indirect cost (indirect cost is overhead).

cost accounting: Recording of cost data and preparation of cost statements.

costs: This term can be discussed in both monetary and non-monetary senses. In general, we say that costs are involved whenever a commodity or service is produced; so that when the owner a factor of production offers its services to a producer the cost to the owner is one of direct consumption foregone; whereas, for the producer, there is a definite, measurable, monetary cost involved in the employment of the services of the factor in the productive process. In the latter type, they are called wages, salaries, rent, and interest.

credit: In general, this means the granting of a period of time by a creditor to a debtor at the expiration of which the later must pay the debt. In book-keeping it means the acknowledgement of payment by a book-entry.

credit card: A judicial card issued to customers authorising the obtaining of goods on credit.

credit control: Any policy, governmental or otherwise, designed to exercise control over the volume of credit, i.e. to keep it constant, contract or expand it.

creditor: Payable. Liability. One to whom a debt is owing; one who gives credit for money or goods.

credit sale: A credit sale differs from a hire purchase agreement in that the parties are buyer and seller, who have entered into agreement (for the sale of goods) under which payment is to be made at a specified time or times after the contract of sale (i.e. the buyer normally gets possession of the goods before he has paid for them). A credit sale is sometimes known as instalment buying.

currency: Anything which is acceptable as a medium of exchange, i.e. as money, can be called currency. It does not have to be legal tender, although the term is frequently used to exclude other forms of money, e.g. cheques and postal orders.

current account: This is a deposit account from which money can be withdrawn at any time. This type of deposit account does not command interest payments.

current asset: Something owned by a business that is either cash or can be turned into a known amount of cash quickly; or is owned with the intention of selling it for cash within one year.

current liability: Liability due for payment within one operating period, normally one year. Does not include long-term liabilities or owners equity.

curve: Line of which no part is straight; line showing diagrammatically a continuous variation of quantity, force, etc., graph.

customs duty: A tax levied on commodities transported from one country to another, i.e. on imports and/or exports. It is more usual for this kind of tariff to be imposed on imports.

DDDD

data: Facts; the raw material of information. A representation of facts, concepts, or instructions in a formalised manner suitable for communication, interpretation, or processing by humans or automatic means.

database: A set of two or more interrelated files, each of which contains at least one element in common. A collection of libraries of data. The cornerstone of a management information system; basic data are commonly defined and consistently organised to fit the information needs of a wide variety of users in an organisation.

database administrator: The person responsible for managing the technical aspects of database design, creation and maintenance in an organisation.

database management system: A software or hardware system that interfaces between the database on a system and users and programs to provide for addition, deletion, modification or retrieval of data elements, records and files by logical reference to them.

data dictionary: A listing of all the data elements available in an organisation which describes each data element and identifies its source, location and uses.

data element: A field within a data record, e.g. name, address, sex, code number, student's number, commodity number, etc.

Jacob W. Chikuhwa

data managers: Also known as data-management packages, these are application software packages that comprise the everyday tasks of recording and filing information.

data processing: One or more operation performed on data to achieve a desired objective. A systematic set of procedures for collecting, manipulating and disseminating data to achieve specific objectives.

death duties: Taxation levies upon the estate of a deceased person. It may take either of two forms: (a) when the gross value of the estate is assessed and taxed before it is divided up between the beneficiaries; and, (b) when what is received by the beneficiaries is taxed. The former is usually called an estate duty; the latter type may be called an inheritance, legacy, or succession tax.

debenture: A document that shows the debenture owner has lent money to the business for a specific period of time, at an annual rate of interest. In some cases the capital sum is secured against certain of the business's assets. A debenture does not necessarily confer any special rights or privileges upon the holder, although it is usually secured in some way.

debit: A book-keeping entry recording an amount owing. See credit.

debt: Something owed by one person, or body, to another.

debt capital: Money loaned to a business for more than one year.

debtor: Receivable. Account received. One who owes money or an obligation or duty.

debt service: The payment of interest on a debt, plus whatever instalments of the principal are due. The term is most commonly used in connection with the national debt.

decentralisation: A term usually applied to the practice of establishing industry away from urban areas and, perhaps, away from other industries.

decentralised data processing: Dispersed data processing with independent computers at local sites.

decision theory: The application of statistical probability theory in deciding the best policy to adopt to achieve an objective.

dedicated machine: A computer that has been specifically adapted to perform specific tasks.

deferred income: (a) Income received in advance of being earned and recognised. Normally left as a theoretical current liability in the balance sheet, until the sale is made and the income recognised. (b) Also referred to as "unearned" income, it is income in the form of rent, interest, dividend or any other form which is not the direct result of the recipient's personal effort, i.e. income from capital and other forms of property.

deferred securities: Securities that rank for dividend only after other forms have been satisfied, i.e. after debenture holders and preference and ordinary shareholders have been paid.

deficit: A deficiency in monetary terms. It usually refers to the amount by which liability exceeds assets, or expenditure exceeds revenue.

deficit financing: This refers to the attempt to alleviate a depression by the deliberate spending, by the State, of more than it received in revenue. This spending will usually be on public works of some kind, so that the State, as an employer, will increase the purchasing power of the community and generate economic activity. The deficit in the national budget can be met by borrowing, or by the printing of more money.

deflation: When the supply of money falls relative to the number of exchange transaction, prices fall and a deflation exists, i.e. incomes have been reduced or are not being spent and the amount of goods and services offered has not contracted to the same extent, with the result that the price level falls.

demand: The demand for an economic good at any time is the amount of it that will be bought at a given price. At different prices, it is likely that different amounts will be bought. For the economist, demand is always effective demand, i.e. the desire to buy must be coupled with the ability to pay.

dependent variable: The terms "dependent variable" and "independent variable" are used in similar but subtly different ways in mathematics and statistics as part of the standard terminology in those subjects. They are used to distinguish between two types of quantities being considered, separating them into those available at the start of a process and those being created by it, where the latter (dependent variables) are dependent on the former (independent variables).

depreciation: Allocation of the cost of a fixed asset to expense over its working life. Measure of the cost of using the fixed asset. Besides being used in connection with capital, it also applies to currency. Depreciation

Jacob W. Chikuhwa

of currency refers to the reduced purchasing power of money, which may be the result of an increase in the supply of money. When the value of a currency in terms of other currencies falls, it is said to have "depreciated".

depression: This is one of the names (the other being slump) given to a period in which business activity is at a low ebb; prices and wages are low; there is a high level of unemployment; little borrowing from the banks; and a general feeling of pessimism amongst businessmen.

devaluation: A downward change in the valuation of one currency in terms of others.

diminishing returns: Also known variously as the law of increasing costs, of non-proportional returns, of diminishing marginal productivity and of diminishing marginal revenue productivity, it postulates that when factors of one or more of those is fixed, then the application of further increments of the other, variable, factor or factors will, at some time, yield diminishing increases in production.

director: Officer of a limited company. Member of the board of directors. Not a partner.

discount: A discount is a deduction from a debt, or a price, or from the face value of something in consideration of prompt or early payment.

disinvestment: A reduction in a stock of capital goods may be called disinvestment. This may occur when producers do not renew worn-out capital or when capital goods are sold.

distributed data processing: Performing operations in a computer system whose terminals and central processing unit (CPU) are separated geographically but are linked together functionally in a communications network, i.e. local processing is carried out by local processors and the results are transmitted to the central computer for further processing.

distribution: The main sense in which the economist uses this term is the apportionment of the national income among the factors of production which co-operate to produce that income. The distribution is then into interest, profit, rent, and wages. Distribution is also used to refer to that part of commerce responsible for the channelling of goods from producers to consumers. In statistics, a distribution is data classified some way, usually in a frequency distribution, which is an arrangement of data showing the frequency with which values occur in certain pre-determined classes or groups, e. g. income groups.

dividend: Sum payable as profit of joint-stock company or to creditors of insolvent estate. A distribution from profits payable at a fixed rate on preference share (see security), or at a varying rate, according to the size of the profits, on ordinary shares.

division of labour: This is an account of specialisation where-by human economic activity becomes increasingly diversified and specialised. It can be seen as part of the process of economic development and its extent may be an index of the state of such development in an economy.

draft: This is a written order relating to a certain sum of money that a creditor wishes paid by a debtor. It usually involves the creditor's banker, who will present it to the debtor for his approval, or acceptance.

duty: Taxation levied upon the import, export or consumption of home-produced commodities. See customs duty and excise duty.

EEEE
earning assets: Assets that earn, e.g. interest earning securities possessed by a firm.

earnings: Income. Profit. Revenue.

economic good: Anything, material or immaterial, that is useful to man, can be obtained and is in some sense scarce. The term is used for all goods which are not free goods.

economic growth: This aspect of economics has increasingly attracted the attention of economists since the Second World War and can be best defined as taking place when there is an increase in the real national product of an economy.

economic law: The word "law" has many meanings, but two are fundamental: a rule, enacted or customary, recognised as binding by a community; or a generalised statement of a particular tendency. An economic law is of the latter kind and is a statement of an invariable relationship between specified economic conditions and phenomena.

economic planning: In general, this refers to any attempt to plan economic activity and anticipate the results. Thus, economic planning is carried on at all levels in the economy although the term is usually used to refer to the governmental direction of economic operations.

Jacob W. Chikuhwa

economics: Definitions of economics fall loosely into two categories: One is based upon wealth and welfare and the other definitions fall within its scope. The more recent category is claimed to be more scientific in its approach, which is from the scarcity of resources to their satisfaction of human wants. In the first category, it is the study of human activities in the ordinary business of life; it investigates how man gets his income and how he uses it. The starting point of the other category of definitions is the recognition of human want and the scarcity of the means to satisfy those wants, i.e. economics is the science which studies human behaviour as a relationship between ends and scarce means which have alternative uses.

economic sanctions: These are economically coercive measures sometimes employed in international affairs in an effort to ensure that decisions collectively made are adhered to.

economic system: The nature of economic life under a particular social system.

economic theory: A body of statements propounding a relationship between economic facts, such facts having been verified by formal investigations of economic activity.

economies of scale: Also known as large-scale production, this is the production of goods on a large scale, i.e. in large quantities. A firm increases its capacity, or scale of production, by increases in the amounts of factors of production in employs, notably capital and labour, and by increases in the efficiency of its factors, e.g. division of labour.

economist: A person expert in economics, or in some branch of the subject.

elasticity of demand: It is possible that within a certain price range, demand may change proportionately with changes in price, i.e. there is a constant relationship between the two. Outside that range, there may be a more than proportionate, or less than proportionate change in demand than in price. A small change in price may produce a big change in demand; or a big change in price produce little or no change in the amount demanded. In the first case, the demand is said to be elastic, and in the second, inelastic.

elasticity of supply: The reaction of supply to a price change will greatly depend upon the nature of the productive process; in particular, the availability of the factors of production. A producer may make a rational decision to increase supply because a higher price is obtainable, but be unable to increase production because the firm is already working at capacity and additional factors are not readily available. In this case there would be an inelasticity of supply. If the productive process is more flexible, then supply will be able to respond to a change in price and supply will be elastic.

employment: In its widest sense, this can mean the use of a factor of production by a firm or government institution. More narrowly, the term refers to the engagement of labour.

end product: A term used to denote that something possessing utility emerges from a productive process.

enterprise: This term is sometimes used interchangeably with firm, but is usually used in the sense of the factor of production which brings together all the other factors and co-ordinates their activities into a productive process, i.e. "management". The function is performed by the entrepreneur.

entrepreneur: The person, or persons, who perform the function of enterprise, i.e. he who makes all the decisions concerning the initiation and conduct of a firm. He bears the risks in business.

equipment: Fixed asset if acquired for long-term use and not for resale. Recorded in the balance sheet at cost less depreciation, not at market value.

equity: The capital of a business that comes from the issue of shares. The goodwill and residual assets of a company after allowing for all liabilities.

ergonomics: This is a study concerned with the output of labour and can be defined as a study of posture and dexterity to obtain maximum efficiency with minimum fatigue.

excess capacity: This means a stock of capital goods that is owned by a firm, but is not in use.

exchange control: This is the control exercised by the State, and usually through the Central (Reserve) Bank, of all dealings in gold and foreign exchange.

Jacob W. Chikuhwa

exchange rate: Strictly, any price is an exchange rate, but the term is invariably used to refer to the price of one currency in terms of another, i.e. the proportion in which two different currencies are exchanged.

excise duty: This is a duty imposed on home-produced goods and domestically provided services. A reason for the imposition of such taxation is to offset or limit the protective effects of the imposition of a customs duty on similar goods imported from abroad.

executive: Having the function of executing. Person in executive position in business organisation, etc. Every knowledge worker in modern organisation is an executive if, by virtue of his position or knowledge, he is responsible for a contribution that materially affects the capacity of the organisation to perform and to obtain results.

expenditure: Money paid for cost, expense, asset or other purpose.

expense: Expenditure properly chargeable in the profit and loss account. Amount used up during the accounting period. Indirect cost. Manufacturing, selling or administrative expense. Includes depreciation of fixed assets.

FFFF

factors of production: Production clearly results from the interaction of various agencies and the economist attempts to classify them. The traditional classification is into the following groups of factors or agents of production: land, labour, capital and enterprise.

file: A set of records relating to a specific business activity. For example, the accounts receivable file of a department store made up of the individual records of the store's credit customers. (See change file, master file, transaction file.)

file handler: A data manager application package which is capable of operating on only one file at a time.

finance: (a) Money resources of State, company or person. (b) Management of money (especially public funds), science of revenue; money support for an undertaking.

finance company: This is a rather vague name that is sometimes applied to firms engaged in hire purchase finance.

finance house: Consumers can obtain credit in various ways, but the most common is through hire purchase. When this method is used, the retailer may finance the transaction himself or he may lodge his hire purchase agreements with a finance house and obtain an advance against them. The customer pays instalments to the retailer, who acts as an agent for the finance house and pays off the advance at a rate based on the instalments due to him.

firm: The production unit, whether it comprises a one-man firm or a large-scale undertaking with thousands of shareholders and employees. A number of firms producing similar goods or services make up an industry; if the firm makes up the industry, a monopoly exists.

fiscal: Concerned with money and credit, particularly public finance.

fiscal policy: Fundamentally, this is the policy pursued by a government for raising the revenue necessary to meet its expenditure. It embraces the scope and degree of taxation, national debt, government borrowing, etc.

fixed assets: Assets such as land, plant and equipment acquired for long-term use in the business and not for resale. Charged to overhead expense periodically as depreciation. Recorded in the balance sheet at cost less depreciation, not market value. Sometimes revalued periodically.

floating assets: Assets that can be quickly converted into cash at or near its book value (sometimes called a "quick" asset).

floppy disk: A flexible disk (diskette) of oxide-coated mylar that is stored in paper or plastic envelopes. The entire envelope is inserted into the disk unit. It is a low-cost random-access form of data storage.

FOB: Free on board: A term referring to the payment for goods when the price does not include charges for insurance and shipment. Compare with CIF.

forecast: Conjectural estimate of something future. A prediction of what the financial position of a business would be in future. Also used in forecasting the weather.

foreign exchange: This is concerned with the exchange of one foreign currency for another. The demand for a foreign currency arises out of indebtedness in international trade; investment in another country; tourism and business travel; speculation concerning changes in exchange rates; and various governmental needs.

free market: A market in which buyers and sellers are free to trade, i.e. in which no compulsion is exercised and no restrictions exist concerning prices and amounts.

Jacob W. Chikuhwa

fringe benefit: A reward received by an employee in addition to the monetary wages paid for actual work done. These benefits are sometimes known as "perks", i.e. casual profit additional to normal revenue or emolument; incidental benefit attaching to employment, etc.

fund: Permanent stock of something ready to be drawn upon; stock of money, especially one set apart for a purpose; (in plural: pecuniary resources.)

GGGG

game theory: The application of statistical logic to competitive situations such as bidding for contracts.

general expense: Expense of the business which is not part of manufacturing, selling, or administrative expense. Sometimes grouped with administrative expense in the income statement. Includes audit fees, legal expense, etc.

gilt-edged securities: These are securities carrying the least amount of risk, and are usually issued by governments.

good: Anything, material or immaterial, exterior to man and useful to him. In fact, a commodity harmful to man but desired by him is a good to the economist.

goodwill: When a business changes hands, continuity of prosperity is likely to be assured if the previous owner, or owners, have built up a good reputation. The probability of such continuity is regarded as an asset of an "intangible" nature, and an assessment of its value will be recorded in a "goodwill account".

government: This is a system of ruling or a form of organisation of a State. An established system of political administration by which a State, district, etc. is governed. All the people who administer or control the affairs of a State, institution, etc.; administration.

government debt: Also referred to as national debt, this is the debt of a central government incurred by expenditure which could not be met out of revenue. This expenditure may be for productive purposes, such as the building of bridges, railways, harbours, roads, etc., or for unproductive purposes, such as war. It is to be noted that when combined with the debts of local government, the total is sometimes called the 'public debt'.

government expenditure: These expenditures form an important part of the aggregate expenditure which, although considered exogenous in the simple income expenditure model, play an important part in this Keynesian model in determining the equilibrium level of the national income. In particular, the government's manipulation of their expenditures, an element of fiscal policy, is considered to be one of the main methods of ensuring that national income is at the full employment national income level.

government securities: The expressions gilt-edged or government bonds, securities or stocks all refer to the securities issued by the government or by nationalised industries and guaranteed by the government.

grant: To give or consider formally or according to legal procedure; to transfer the title of a thing to another by deed or writing. This is also something granted, as property, a tract of land, an executive right or power, money from a fund, etc. A conveyance in writing of such things as cannot pass or be transferred by word only, as land, rents, reversions, titles, etc. The instrument of such conveyance.

gross: A total without deductions, not net.

gross income: An income before any deduction has been made, e.g. for a firm it would represent total receipts before the subtraction of the costs or expenses of production; for an individual, his income before the deduction of income tax.

gross domestic product: This is a measure of a country's overall economic output. It is the market value of all final goods and services made within the borders of a country in a year. It is often positively correlated with the standard of living, though its use as a stand-in for measuring the standard of living has come under increasing criticism and many countries are actively exploring alternative measures to GDP for that purpose.

gross national product: Annual total value of goods produced and services provided in a country.

gross profit: Difference between sales and cost of goods sold. Profit computed before charging for selling and administrative expenses, etc.

ground rent: Rent, in the commercial sense, that is paid to a landlord for the use of land without improvements. The payment of ground rent

Jacob W. Chikuhwa

gives the lessee the right to improve the land (e.g. build on it) and occupy it. (See rent)

HHHH

hard copy: A printed output, a copy of machine output in readable form.

hardware: The physical equipment used in data processing; in electronic data processing, the machine devices in a computer system, including the central processing unit (CPU), devices for data preparation, data input, secondary storage, and output, and devices for intercommunication among hardware components.

high-level language: A programming language oriented towards the problem to be solved or the procedures to be used. English-like coding schemes that are procedure-, problem-, and user-oriented. Such languages include BASIC, COBOL, FORTRAN, Pascal, PL/1, Fourth-generation programming languages (4GLs), etc.

hire purchase: A hire purchase agreement is a hiring of goods coupled with an option to purchase. The hirer is not a person who has bought or agreed to buy goods and, therefore, he cannot pass goods title to a third party. When goods are selected by a consumer who wishes to hire purchase, the dealer immediately sells the goods to a finance house, industrial bank, etc. with which the hirer (i.e. the consumer) enters into a contract of hire purchase. Under the agreement, the hirer undertakes to pay to the owner instalments as specified in the contract. The consumer is not the buyer until he has paid all instalments and then exercises his "option to purchase". The dealer may have sufficient resources to finance the hire purchase himself.

hoarding: The accumulation of goods not intended for immediate consumption. In the case of money, this is hoarded when it is accumulated and put to no use at all, namely it goes out of circulation and the effective supply of money is reduced.

holding company: A company owning a sufficient amount of the securities of another company to control it. This type of firm can hide its real size and occupy the apex of a huge pyramid of the other companies.

host computer: The controlling computer in a computer system.

IIII

imperfect competition: A state of competition in which there is imperfection because of influential positions held by buyers or sellers or both. Thus, in a market situation wherein prices can be abnormally influenced, perfect competition cannot exist. This may be called monopolistic competition.

incentive: This is loosely used to describe a device intended to urge labour to greater productive efforts.

income: Earnings. Profit. Revenue. Sometimes used to mean sales and all forms of incoming benefits, not necessarily in cash. The monetary or non-monetary return to a factor of production as reward for productive activity.

income statement: Profit and loss account.

income tax: This is usually taken to mean a tax on the incomes of individuals. However, the term often embraces the incomes of companies, in which guise it may be called a companies tax.

independent variable: See dependent variable.

index number: A device for measuring the change that has taken place in a group of related items over a period of time, e.g. the price index or the Stock Exchange index. The usual practice is to choose a "base year" and assign to it the value 100. It is then possible to show subsequent percentage changes in prices, costs, production, etc.

industrial relations: The relationships between workers and their employers. See conciliation.

industry: This term is almost exclusively used in a collective sense: a group of firms producing identical or similar products or products having raw materials or uses in common; or more widely to all productive activity in a given area. Often "industry" is used in a sense that precludes commerce, but, strictly, "trading" in productive activity and it is possible to refer to, say, the retail industry.

inflation: General increase of prices and fall in purchasing value of money, increase in available currency resulting in this. Basically, a situation in which prices are rising and pressures exist to accentuate the fall in the value of money. If, for example, incomes increase and this increase in the volume of money available for exchange transactions is not required by or followed by an appropriate expansion in the number

Jacob W. Chikuhwa

of transactions, then a situation exists in which prices will tend to rise. Should income spending fall (or hoarding increase) and the number of exchange transactions fall even more, then a similar tendency exists.

information: Data that has been organised and processed so that they are meaningful. Communicated knowledge expressed in a form that makes it immediately useful for decision making.

infrastructure: An economy's capital in the form of roads, railways, water supplies, educational facilities, health services, etc., without which investment in factories, machinery, tools, etc., cannot be fully productive. Its characteristics are that it is often self-liquidating and has a high capital-output ratio, i.e. the relationship between a given increase in investment and the associated increase in output.

insurance: An arrangement whereby one party (the insurer) agrees, in return for a premium, to provide indemnity for another party (the insured) in the event of some specified loss. Insurance is protection against such risks as accidents, fire, crop failure, the advent of twins, ill health, etc.

intangible assets: Assets of no material substance, e.g. goodwill, high workers' morale, good relations with banks, etc.

intelligent terminal: A terminal with an internal processor that can be programmed to perform specified functions, such as data editing, data conversion and control of other terminals.

interest: A sum, usually expressed as a "rate" or percentage, paid for the use of capital. The classical view of interest is that it is a reward for saving, a payment for the risk and trouble involved in making a loan, a cost of investment and that the rate is determined by the interaction of the demand for loans and the supply of loanable funds.

inventory: Stock. Detailed list of goods, furniture, raw materials, etc.

inventory modelling: Determines the stock-holding levels and re-order quantities that give minimum overall stockholding costs.

investment: Amount invested in stocks, shares, bonds debentures or any asset. In other words, it is the conversion of monetary resources into liquid resources (wealth).

investment trust: Investment trusts are companies which use their resources to buy securities of various kinds with the object of distributing the income therefrom to their shareholders.

issue: An issue is a block of securities being sold by a company. The term is also applied to the offer for sale and allotment of the securities to the public.

issued capital: Share capital actually issued by a company. Part of owner's equity in the balance sheet.

issuing house: An issuing house acts as an agent between those seeking long-term capital and those willing to provide it. Its function is essentially to act as sponsors and underwriters rather than as a source of finance.

JJJJ

jobber: This term sometimes refers to a merchant middlemen who buys from a manufacturer or importer and sells to wholesalers or retailers. But its more familiar meaning is a dealer in securities on a Stock Exchange who buys and sells from and to other members of the exchange.

joint demand: The demand which exists when two or more economic goods must be used together, i.e. joint demand is the composite of the demands for goods which are used at, or nearly at, the same time. For example, the building of a house means a joint demand for bricks, sand, cement, timber, glass, etc.

joint stock: Capital held jointly. The joint ownership by a group of people of a business or firm, usually referred to as a public joint-stock company. See limited company.

joint supply: The supply of two or more economic goods which are produced together, e.g. beef, hide and glue; wool, mutton and catgut; corn and straw. One product may be a by-product of the other.

KKKK

key: A unique identifier for a record; used to sort records for processing or to locate a particular record within a file.

keypunch: A keyboard device that punches holes in a card to represent data.

keypunch operator: A data-entry operator that uses a keypunch to transcribe data in a form suitable for computer processing.

Jacob W. Chikuhwa

key transcription: The creation of a machine-sensible medium by operators using machines with typewriter-like keyboards to punch data into cards or paper tape to encode data on magnetic tape or disks.

keyword: A primary element in a programming language statement.

kilobyte: A kilobyte equals 2^{10} or 1 024 bytes and is commonly abbreviated as "K" and used as a suffix when describing memory size. N.B. byte = 8 bits (a bit (binary digit) is represented by the presence or absence of an electronic pulse, 0 or 1)

LLLL

labour: The factor of production comprising all human economic effort, mental and physical, skilled or unskilled, applied to the production of wealth (i.e. creation of utility) and in receipt of reward for the effort.

labour theory of value: This theory states that the value of an economic good derives solely from the amount of labour embodied in it. Labour is, therefore, considered as the source and measure of value.

labour turnover: Also known as manpower turnover, it is the number of workers who leave a firm compared with the number engaged to replace them during a specific period of time.

land: Freehold or leasehold property owned by a business. Normally fixed asset. Recorded at cost. One of the traditional factors of production.

legal tender: Any form of money which is a legal quittance of a debt, i.e. money which, according to law, must be accepted as payment of any obligation stated in monetary terms.

letter of credit: An order in writing from a banker to his agent abroad, or to another banker abroad, to authorise payment to the person named in the letter of a specific sum, or amounts not in total exceeding that sum.

limited company: Company whose shareholders have limited their liability to the amounts they subscribed to the shares they hold, i.e. limited liability. In other words, a shareholder cannot be held personally liable to a company's debts beyond the fully paid-up value of the securities he holds.

limited partnership: A type of partnership in which the principle of limited liability is extended to the holdings of non-active partners in the enterprise.

linear programming: A mathematical device for determining the best way to allocate a limited amount of resources. In a linear programming problem, all the relationships are expressed as linear or straight line, function.

liquid: If something is "liquid" it is easily converted into cash without appreciable loss in value. Liquid assets, the most liquid being cash and bank deposits, are clearly the opposite of "illiquid", or frozen, assets such as buildings and land, which may be difficult to sell quickly without loss in value.

liquidation: The dissolution or winding-up of a business, i.e. the conversion of its assets into cash, the settlement of any indebtedness there may be and the distribution among the owners of any funds remaining.

liquidity: Availability of cash or assets easily turned into cash.

lock-out: An industrial dispute in which the employer closes down the firm in an attempt to bring the workers to terms. See strikes.

long-term liability: Liability not due for payment within one year. Bonds, debentures or loans. Holders are creditors and receive interest. They are not shareholders.

loss: Opposite of profit or income. Excess of costs and expenses over sales.

low-level language: Any programming language that is more similar to machine language than human language, e.g. machine code and assembly code.

MMMM
machinery: Fixed asset if acquired for use and not for resale. Valued at cost less depreciation. Machinery manufactured or acquired for resale in inventory.

macroeconomics: That part of the subject dealing with broad aggregates of economic entities, e.g. total production, consumption, employment, in come, general price levels, etc. Macroeconomics is not concerned with

Jacob W. Chikuhwa

the detailed workings of an economy, which are investigated by microeconomics.

magnetic disk: A storage medium consisting of a metal platter coated on both sides with magnetic recording material upon which data are stored in the form of magnetised spots; suitable for direct (random) processing.

magnetic drum: A cylinder with a magnetic outer surface on which data are stored.

magnetic tape: A storage medium consisting of a narrow strip upon which spots of iron-oxide are magnetised to represent data; a sequential (serial) storage medium.

maintenance cost: Expense of maintain or repairing the fixed assets of the business. Charged as expense in the income statement.

management information system: MIS is a formal network that extends computer use beyond reporting and into the area of management decision-making; its goal is to get the correct information to the appropriate manager at the right time.

manufacturing expense: Overheads for manufacturing. Part of cost of goods sold.

margin: In the commercial and financial sense, an extra amount beyond that necessary, a precautionary additional amount, etc. It is also the additional cover for speculative investments in which sense the stockbroker provides that part of the cost of the investments which is not financed by the investor and the margin is the difference between the amount of the loan and the current value of the securities deposited as collateral security for the laon. This is "buying on margin".

marginal cost: The additional increase in total cost resulting from the production of one more unit of output.

marginal product: The increase in total output that results from the use of one more increment of a variable factor of production in conjunction with other fixed factors.

marginal productivity: The ability of one more unit of a variable factor of production to increase total output when used in conjunction with other, fixed, factors.

marginal revenue: The increase in total revenue resulting from the sale of one more unit of output.

market: (a) Gathering of people for purchase and sale of provisions, livestock, etc. (b) Open space or covered building in which provisions, cattle, etc., are exposed for sale. (c) Demand for commodity or service; place where there is such demand, e.g. money or capital market. Benham described this as "any area over which buyers and sellers are in such close touch with one another, either directly or through dealers, that the prices obtainable in one part of the market affect the prices paid in other parts".

market price or value: Under conditions of perfect competition, the market price is that at which the amount of a good or service offered by sellers just equals the quantity that will be accepted by the buyers. When these quantities are unequal, i.e. supply is greater thjan demand, or vice versa, then the market price will be lower, or higher, respectively.

market trend: The general, long-term movement of prices of securities in the Stock Exchange.

mark-up: The gross profit that an article would yield if sold at the normal or expected price. Or, the difference between the total cost of production and the selling price, i.e. the cost of distribution.

master file: The file containing primary and relatively permanent records for an application, e.g. the complete set of permanent records for credit customers of a department store is the master file for the accounts receivable system.

maturity: When applied to commercial bills and securities, the date on which repayment of the principal is due.

median: This is the value of the mid-point of a distribution, i.e. there are as many values greater than it as there are values smaller.

memorandum of association: A document required from every joint-stock company at the time of its formation, stating its powers, objects and conditions of incorporation.

merchant bank: The origins of this type of business are in the ordinary buying and selling of goods; business to which has been added a range of financial services, including acceptance. Merchant banks tend to specialise in certain classes of business, but nearly all of them have made the acceptance of commercial bills a vital part of their activities. All do some ordinary banking business, a substantial part of their deposits coming from other banks and companies abroad. Like the joint-

Jacob W. Chikuhwa

stock banks, insurance companies and some other institutions, the merchant banks act as trustees and as investment advisers.

microcomputer: A computer built around a microprocessor by adding circuitry and devices to provide memory, input/output, and control functions.

microeconomics: The part of economics concerned with the detailed workings (nitty-gritty) of the economy, i.e. the study of particular cases, such as labour turnover, productivity, supply and demand trends, etc.

microfilm: A spool of film for recording data and documents in greatly reduced size. The recorded images must be magnified in order to be read.

microprocessor: The CPU of a microcomputer. An integrated circuit that will perform a variety of operations in accordance with a set of instructions.

minicomputer: A size category of computers that overlaps both microcomputers on the small end and mainframes on the larger end. It tends to have smaller word sizes than a mainframe and larger word sizes than a microcomputer. Its instruction set tends to be larger than that of a microcomputer but smaller than that of a mainframe.

minimum wage: A minimum wage level, usually established by law, to be paid to the employee in certain occupations or industries. The minimum may be agreed upon as the result of collective bargaining.

mixed economy: An economy containing the characteristics of both capitalism and socialism, i.e. a combination of private and public ownership of the means of production, with some measure of control by the central government.

mode: This is the value of the most frequent score in a distribution.

model: A mathematical system used to describe the workings of part or the whole of an economy.

monetary policy: This refers to the use of certain monetary controls by a government to regulate economic activity. They include restriction or expansion of the supply of money and manipulation of the interest rates in order to make borrowing cheaper of dearer, or easier or more difficult to obtain.

money: A commodity accepted by common consent as a means of exchange, a medium in which prices are expressed, a circulation medium to facilitate exchange and measure wealth. It is possible to distinguish four major functions performed by money: (a) A "medium of exchange", an intermediate selected commodity, whereby goods and services are paid for and debts and other contracts discharged. (b) A measure of value, a unit of account, a common denominator of value in which records are kept, costs calculated and prices stated. (c) A "standard for deferred payments", i.e. a basis for credit transactions so that when payment is to be made at a future date, the exact extent of the obligation is known. (d) A store of value or "reserve of ready purchasing power", i.e. a means of conserving purchasing power.

money market: A market that facilitates the borrowing and lending of short-term funds (i.e. two to three years to maturity).

monopoly: The most extreme departure from perfect competition. It assumes a market in which there is only one seller of a commodity, i.e. where there is a single control over the supply of a good or service and that control can be maintained.

mortgage: Long-term loan secured on a fixed asset. Long-term liability. This is a conditional conveyance of land or other property as security for the performance of some condition, e.g. the payment of debt; becoming void once the condition has been performed, i.e. on repayment of debt the property is re-conveyed to the debtor.

multiprogramming: A technique whereby several programs are placed in primary storage at the same time, giving the illusion that they are being executed simultaneously; this results in increased CPU active time.

NNNN

national debt: This is the debt of a central government incurred by expenditure which could not be met out of revenue. This expenditure may be for productive purposes, such as the building of bridges, railways, harbours, roads, etc., or for unproductive purposes such as war.

national income: The total net earnings received by the factors of production (i.e. wages + profit + interest + rent) for their productive effort in an economy and for a specific period of time. This is also called "national income at factor cost".

Jacob W. Chikuhwa

national product: The value of the goods and services produced by an economy during a given period. As the product of a producing unit in a given period must be exactly the same value as the sum of the incomes of the factors of production which gave rise to that product, then national product must equal national income. These are also equal to the national outlay as the total expenditure on the consumption of commodities and services plus sums expended on capital goods must equal both the total product and the total incomes.

national resources: This term is identical in meaning with that of land, i.e. the wealth freely supplied by nature.

national wealth: The total value, in monetary terms, of all the economic goods possessed by the members of an economy at a specified time. The national wealth would, therefore, exclude economic goods owned by foreigners.

net: (a) Figure after deduction, e.g. gross sales less sales returns, equals net sales. (b) Payment of full amount with no allowance for cash discount.

net assets: The assets attributable to the share capital after deducting external liabilities including the future taxation reserve and the nominal value of any debentures, added to any premium payable on them and any arrears of interest.

net asset worth: A measurement of the value of ordinary shares, which is calculated by dividing the net equity assets by the number of such shares.

net equity assets: The net assets minus the repayment value of the preference capital (see securities) including arrears of preference dividends.

net investments: Investment after providing for depreciation and the replacement of capital.

net national debt: The total national debt after deducting that part of it held by the government in sinking funds, etc.

net profit: Profit for the accounting period after income tax. Net income. Net earnings. Increase owner's equity. In other words, it is the residue left from gross profit after the deduction of selling and operating expenses (including depreciation charges, auditors' and directors' fees, interest payments, etc.).

net profit margin: Net profit expressed as a percentage of turnover.

net issue: The issue of securities which are offered to the public either directly, or through brokers, by companies themselves, or on their behalf by an issuing house.

nominal income: Money wages, nominal wages or national income is the actual amount, in monetary units, received as income. See real income.

nominal value: This, also called nominal share value is the face value of securities, such as ordinary shares, preference shares (securities), etc.

nominal yield: The rate of return, usually expressed as a percentage, on securities calculated on their nominal value.

normal price: When the amount of a good or service offered by sellers in a market is not equal to the quantity that will be accepted by buyers (i.e. demand), then there will be a market price higher or lower than it would be if supply and demand were equal. The existence of a higher price may have the effect of either contracting demand or expanding supply, and vice versa, with the result that it can be assumed that eventually there will be an equilibrium between supply and demand. At this point, there will be an equilibrium, or normal price, sometimes called normal value. See also supply and demand.

normal profit: A valuable concept in economic theory which enables us to consider a cost for the entrepreneur. Normal profit is the minimum income that the entrepreneur will accept, i.e. the least reward he will accept in return for the entrepreneurial contribution to production. See profit.

normal value: Face value of shares. Authorised and issued share capital in the balance sheet shows the nominal value of the shares separately from any premium or discount.

OOOO

official list: The list of dealings and prices in the Stock Exchange published at the end of each day's business.

oligopoly: A departure from perfect competition in which there are only a few producers of a good or service. This commodity produced may be homogeneous, in which case the oligopoly may be called "perfect", or there may be product differentiation, in which case the industry may be

Jacob W. Chikuhwa

called "imperfect oligopoly". Oligopoly is sometimes called "partial monopoly".

on-line: Pertaining to equipment or devices physically attached to and under the direct control of a CPU. Also refers to data processing activities performed on the computer.

on-line processing system: A system where people and equipment are in direct communication with the CPU of a computer.

opening stock: Inventory at the beginning of the accounting period.

open market operations: The buying or selling of securities in the open market by a Central (Reserve) Bank for the purpose of curtailing or expanding the volume of credit. By selling securities, the Central Bank can absorb funds, and by buying them, it can release funds into the money market.

operating expenses: All overheads of the business. Sometimes restricted to mean only selling, administrative and general expenses.

operating system: An organised collection of software available to the computer at all times, that controls the overall operations of a computer.

Operational Research: The application of mathematical techniques to a wide variety of management problems.

optimum: This is achieved when the most favourable economic conditions apply.

order: Purchase order to a supplier for delivery of goods and services.

organisation: An organised body. A social artefact. Not a biological organism, but like an amoeba, is in constant, direct contact with the environment. It is an organ of society and fulfils itself by the contribution it makes to the outside environment.

output: The amount of good or service, or both, produced by a producing unit, i.e. by a firm, an industry or an economy.

overdraft: A loan facility granted by a bank to a customer, whereby he is permitted to draw upon his account (to overdraw) beyond the amount deposited therein and up to an agreed amount. See credit.

overhead: Overhead expense. Indirect cost which cannot be conveniently associated with a unit of production.

over-subscribed issue: An issue for which application to buy are in excess of securities available.

owner's equity: Owner's claim. Amount due to owners of the business, increased by profits, reduced by losses and dividends. (Computed: assets less liabilities equal owner's equity.)

PPPP

paid-up capital: See capital.

parameter: This is a statistic relating to a population.

parity: Equality; a "parity of exchange" meaning the ratio at which things are exchangeable. The term is most used in connection with currencies, in which case it is an agreed, fixed exchange rate for a currency.

partnership: When two or more people agree to carry on a business together intending to share the profits. This is usually created through a contractual agreement as opposed to a Memorandum of Association required for the creation of a joint-stock company. Partners have equal powers and responsibilities and each is jointly liable with his co-partners for all the debts and obligations of the firm.

patent: Legal right to exploit an invention. Asset in the balance sheet. Recorded at cost less depreciation under the heading "other assets".

payable: Creditor. Liability. Account payable.

pegging: This term is used when an attempt is made to maintain a price or rate, or to keep it within close limits. The term is often applied to intervention in a foreign exchange market by the authorities to restrict the movement of exchange rates.

perfect competition: An important concept in economic theory that acts as a limiting case, departures from which include imperfect competition, monopoly and oligopoly. Perfect completion is the opposite of monopoly.

perpetual debenture: A debenture with no maturity date, the interest being paid indefinitely.

personnel: A body of persons employed in a company (firm), government or any public undertaking (local authority).

piecework: A method of paying wages, whereby payment depends upon the amount produced by the individual worker.

plant: Equipment and machinery. Fixed asset if acquired for use and not for resale.

Jacob W. Chikuhwa

plough back: The re-investment of profits made by companies in themselves, i.e. the profit is not distributed, but used to buy capital goods such as buildings, machinery, etc.

population: The population or universe, is the totality of items in a statistical investigation. If all the items are used, the study is called a census; otherwise samples are taken.

portfolio: A list of securities.

potential demand: A demand expected at some future date. For example, if the power to purchase is increasing, or cuts in taxation are expected, the "potential demand" becomes "effective demand".

premium: A payment for insurance cover; or a payment for a loan in lieu of, or in addition to, interest; or the amount by which a currency or a security stands above its issue price, i.e. the excess of the market price over the par, or paid-up value of the securities. In the case of currency, it would be the excess of the market price (i.e. exchange rate) over an official rate, or normally ruling rate.

price: An estimation of the value of an economic good in terms of money.

price fixing: An administrative fixing of price levels; also called "price control".

primary storage: Also known as internal storage or main storage (memory), this is the section of the CPU that holds instructions, data and intermediate and final results during processing.

principal: Money of which interest is paid.

printer: A device used to produce permanent (hard-copy) computer outputs; impact printers are designed to work mechanically; non-impact printers use heat, laser, or chemical technology.

probability: The likelihood that a specific event will occur. In statistics, a numerical value is used to state probability, e.g. three chances in a thousand, 0,997 or 99,7%.

probability distribution: A series of probabilities corresponding to all the values of the variables which are possible. It can be regarded as a frequency distribution standardised in such a way that the total frequency (i.e. number of values) is one.

product: The result of production.

production: Producing. Production involves creating "things", as when a manufacturer converts cotton thread into cloth. But the making of things is as such irrelevant to economic production. For the economist, all activities must be included which yield useful results, whether they are embodied in material objects or not. The dry-cleaners who clean our clothes are as much "producers" as the tailor who sews them or the manufacturer who produces cloth.

productivity: The amount produced by a factor of production in a given period of time; the efficiency with which productive resources are used; or the relationship between physical resources used in production and the units of output produced in a specified period of time.

profit: Income. Excess of sales over costs and expenses, during an accounting period. Does not necessarily increase cash; it may be reflected in increased assets or decreased liabilities.

profit and loss account: Income statement. Not a balance sheet. Statement showing sales, costs, expenses and profit for an accounting period.

profit before tax: Operating profit less non-operating expenses plus non-operating income, in the income statement.

profit-sharing: A system of remuneration of labour in which a bonus in proportion to net profit (in the commercial sense under profit) is given in addition to wages.

programmer: A person whose job it is to design, write, and test computer programs.

programming: The process of translating a problem from its physical environment to a language that a computer can understand and obey.

promissory note: An unconditional promise in the form of a document made by one person to another, signed by the maker, engaging to pay on demand, or at the fixed or determinable future time, a sum certain in money, to, or to the order of, a specified person or to bearer.

prospectus: A document, subject to strict legal requirements, in which details are given of securities to be offered for sale.

protection: The policy of imposing tariffs on imported goods in order to protect domestic industries.

public finance: The financial operations of central and local government.

Jacob W. Chikuhwa

public good: An economic good supplied, without direct payment, to people by the government, e.g. parks, museums, libraries, education, etc.

public utility: An industry, such as gas, electricity, water and transport facilities, which requires heavy and highly specialised initial investment of capital, on which the return is slow. These are essential public services, the supply of which would not be necessarily forthcoming from private enterprise.

public works: The building of roads, bridges, canals, public baths and parks, and other public construction projects designed to increase the welfare of the community.

published financial statements: Balance sheet, profit and loss account and statement of accumulated profit, with comparative figures and notes disclosing the information required under the Companies Act.

punched card: An out-dated form of sequential storage in which data is represented by the presence or absence of strategically placed holes.

purge: In data processing, to remove inactive or unused records from a master file.

QQQQ

quality control: The use of statistical theory and techniques to record and check on the measurable qualities of products and processes.

queue: A list or collection of programs waiting for execution by the CPU; normally ordered on a first-in, first-out basis.

queuing theory: A mathematical technique for solving problems caused by waiting lines wherever they may occur.

quotas: The allotment to individuals, firms or countries of maximum permitted quantities of goods. The term is frequently used in connection with imports, so that an "import quota" is quantitative restriction imposed on goods entering a country.

quotation: In the Stock Exchange, this refers both to the privilege granted by the council of having the price of a security appear in the official list, and to the two prices quoted by the jobber, when he is approached by a stock-broker.

RRRR

R and D: Research and Development cost. Normally expense. Sometimes treated as "other assets".

random access: This is when data can be retrieved directly without the need for sorting. See magnetic disk.

random variable: A numerical variable which can take different values with different proportions.

range: A measure of dispersion that is simply the difference between the smallest and the largest values in a distribution.

raw material: A resource prior to production, during which process its nature is changed. In data processing, the term is used to refer to raw data, i.e. figures that need rearranging (processing) into information. (See information.)

real income: As opposed to nominal income (the actual sum of money received as income), real income refers to the purchasing power of that income. Real income, thus, takes into account changes in prices, i.e. in the value of money.

real-time data processing system: (a) A processing system that feeds back information in time to effect the situation from which the raw data were generated. (b) A processing system that meets sever time constraints in updating the master file and/or in proving response. (c) Loosely, any processing system featuring on-line data entry with immediate update and/or instantaneous response.

receivable: Account receivable. Debtor. Current asset.

recession: The term given to a falling-off in business activity. It could be a temporary phenomenon, but could continue into a depression.

redeemable: Capable of being recovered, or freed, by payment. All debts are normally redeemable, as are most securities (redeemable preference shares, debentures, and most government securities).

redemption: Recovery, usually by payment. The redemption of a debt is the payment of the amount borrowed. The "redemption date" is the date on which redemption must take place. (See maturity.)

redundancy: This means the superabundance of a factor of production, product, etc. It is almost exclusively used to refer to labour for which there is no employment, i.e. labour dismissed for reasons other than misconduct.

Jacob W. Chikuhwa

regression: This analysis attempts to establish the sort of relationship that might exist between two variables, so that values of one may be predicted from given values of the other.

remote job entry: Remote job entry or "remote batch processing" is a technique which enables batch processing to be employed by remote operating units by sharing a centrally located computer.

remote processing: The processing of computer programs through an input/output device that is remotely connected to a computer system.

rent: In ordinary usage, rent usually means an amount paid for the hire of a house, a plot of land, a television set, etc., a periodical payment for the use of something.

replacement costs: A term sometimes used in connection with the valuation of a firm's assets. The replacement costs are the costs of replacing old capital goods with new ones capable of performing the same functions.

replacement theory: Applied when deciding the best point of time to replace equipment subject to wear and tear in order to minimise the probability of sudden failure and also to minimise replacement costs.

reserve: A fund held for some special purpose or future occasion. A company, for example, will plough back the accumulated reserves, which become the amount by which assets exceed paid-up capital and liabilities. Undervaluation of assets by a firm builds up a "hidden reserve".

retail: To sell to consumers, usually in small quantities. A firm which does this is called a "retailer". See wholesaler.

retained earnings: Accumulated profit. Available for dividend. Part of owner's equity.

revaluation: The restoration of a value lost by devaluation.

revenue: Earnings. Income. Profit. Sometimes also used to mean sales. This is not used to describe the funds received by individuals. The most common use is in public finance, i.e. the income received by government from rates, taxation, duties, etc.

revival: The period when an economy is recovering from a depression.

rights issue: An offer of new shares that gives preferential terms to existing shareholders.

SSSS

salary: A name sometimes given to wages when paid to workers of a certain status (e.g. executive, professional, etc.) at intervals longer than a week.

sales: Total of amounts sold. Recognised normally when goods are shipped to customers.

sales expense: Cost of promoting sales and retaining customers. Indirect cost. Overhead expense.

sample: A selection of data from a population.

sampling frame: A description of a population in the form of a list, map, etc., from which a sample may be drawn.

saving: Saving is abstinence from consumption, an exchange of present income against an equal amount of income in the future, or against the security accompanying a store of wealth. See also investment.

savings banks: These are banks which accept small deposits, on which low rates of interest are paid and which are withdrawable at relatively short notice. Cheque facilities are not normally given to depositors.

scarcity value: Where the demand exceeds the supply of an economic good and the market price is high in consequence, the commodity or service is said to have scarcity value.

scatter diagram: An alternative method used for forecasting financial requirements. Also called simple regression method, it is a graphic portrayal of joint relations.

schedule: Usually a table listing quantities dependent on two variable influences. For example, demand and supply schedules and liquidity preference schedules, in which are listed the various amounts of money demanded at different interest rates.

secondary storage: Also known as external, or auxiliary, or backing storage; supplements primary storage, but operates at slower speeds.

securities: Assets claimable by some creditors in priority to others. Collateral. A security is a document entitling its rightful holder to money, goods or property. The commonest use of the term is for certificates issued to someone who has made some form of investment, for which payments are made. (See dividend and interest.)

self-liquidating: An investment the original cost of which is paid for out of its earnings.

Jacob W. Chikuhwa

seller's market: A market condition in which prices are high, i.e. favourable to sellers. Such a condition is usually a reflection of scarcity (see scarcity value), i.e. when demand exceeds supply, and buyers wish to acquire goods or services even if they have to pay a high price. See buyers' market.

serial access: This is when records can only be accessed serially, i.e. it is necessary to read all records until the one required is reached. See magnetic tape.

service: A non-material economic good produced by a person, firm or industry for the benefit of another, e.g. teachers, musicians, artists and clergymen produce services. Services, as compared with material economic goods, are generally consumed as they are produced.

share: Also known as share certificate, it is a document certifying ownership of shares in a company. Part of owner's equity.

share capital: Capital stock. Part of owner's equity. Money put into a business by the owners.

shareholder: Owner of part of the share capital and owner's equity. One who holds a share certificate, i.e. who has legal title to shares (see securities). Stockholder.

share index: A number of bonds, stocks or shares (see securities) are selected from a list of various trades or businesses and their market prices are added together to make up the base of the index number.

short bonds: Short bonds, or "shorts", are gilt-edged securities having less than five years to run to maturity.

significance test: A significance test is a method of evaluating the likelihood that the difference between numerical observations can be attributed to chance or not.

simple interest: Interest that is calculated upon the original sum, the principal, but not on any interest earned by it.

simulation: The representation of features of behaviour of a physical or abstract system by the behaviour of another system, e.g. the representation of physical phenomena by means of a set of mathematical functions or by operations performed by a computer.

sinking fund: A fund into which sums are put periodically in order that they and the accumulated interest will eventually pay off a debt or replace an asset.

sleeping partner: One who puts capital into a partnership but does not intend to take an active part in running the business. See limited company, limited partnership.

social accounting: This describes the macro-economic — national income field. The economic activities of production, consumption, saving, investment spending and earning are all performed by persons, households, firms, committees, institutions, charities, government bodies, etc. Each of these units keeps an account of its transactions in some form or other and these make up social or national accounts.

social economics: This can be described as a branch of applied economics, which studies the social causes and consequences of economic behaviour.

soft copy: Data displayed on a CRT screen; not a permanent record; contrast with hard copy.

software: A general term for computer programs, procedural rules, and the documentation involved in the operation of a computer system. In other words, these are programs used to direct the computer for problem solving and overseeing operations.

sole trader: Simplest type of business. No shareholders, just the owner's money and borrowings.

source document: An original document from which basic data is extracted, e.g. invoice, sales slip, inventory tag, etc.

specialisation: This means a differentiation to adapt to changed conditions; an intensification of the activity of economic forces in order that production should be increased, i.e. a more economic use of the factors of production. The factor which usually receives most attention in this respect is labour, but there are many other kinds of specialisation: of processing; of geographical areas in extractive and manufacturing industries; in ancillary services such as banking, insurance and transport; and in ancillary trades making components for assembly industries.

speculation: The buying and selling of goods with the object of gaining from differences in prices. Buying at a low price to sell later at a higher price, and selling at a high price in anticipation of being able to buy at a lower price before delivery must be made, are the essential forms of speculation.

Jacob W. Chikuhwa

stabilisation: Generally, this refers to the prevention of fluctuations in economic phenomena. For example, price stabilisation means keeping the price level steady; business stabilisation would mean the avoidance of the trade cycle; and wage stabilisation keeping wage rates from varying too much. (See wages policy.)

stamp duty: A tax, imposed by the State and collected through the purchase of stamps which are required to be affixed to certain documents.

standard deviation: The most important measure of dispersion. It is the square root of the variance of a distribution, the variance being the arithmetic mean of the squared differences (or deviations) of individual values from their mean. It is sometimes called the "root-mean-square-deviation".

standard error: It is assumed that statistics (e.g. arithmetic mean, standard deviation, etc.) of samples taken from the same population are distributed in a normal curve. The standard deviation of this curve is called the standard error.

standard of living: A concept denoting the amount of material well-being to which a social group is accustomed.

statistical regularity, law of: This states that a sample of data taken at random from a larger group, namely a population, tends to reproduce the characteristics of the larger group.

statistics: (a) Numerical facts systematically collected (statistics of population, crime, telephone faults, etc.). (b) Science of collecting, classifying, and using statistics, especially in or for large quantities or numbers. This discipline may be defined as the measurement, enumeration or estimation of natural or social phenomena, systematically arranged so as to exhibit their inter-relation. The technique used for assembling and analysing the data is called statistical method.

stock: Inventory. Goods on hand for resale or manufacture. Stores. Raw material, work in progress, finished goods. Valued at the lower of manufacturing cost or market value.

stockbroker: A broker who is a member of a Stock Exchange, buying and selling securities on behalf of clients (or himself) for a commission.

stock exchange: A market in securities which facilitates the investment of funds and the subsequent liquidation of such investments. Capital would have less mobility if Stock Exchanges did not exist; individuals or corporate bodies with funds to invest would be reluctant to do so if difficulty was likely to be experienced afterwards in converting the securities back into money. Stock Exchanges mostly deal in "second-hand securities", i.e. the buying and selling is of securities already owned by someone else, who may, or may not, have been the original investor.

stockpiling: The accumulation of materials regarded as being vital to national, or international defence.

straight line depreciation: Depreciation method charging off the cost of a fixed asset equally over the years of its working life.

strikes: A strike is a concerted stoppage of work as a protest against wages, hours of work, conditions of work, unfair treatment of a worker, or some other dissatisfaction.

subscription price: The price at which a new issue may be purchased. This price often differs from both the nominal value of the securities and the market price subsequently established.

subsidiary company: A company subject to the control of another company usually because the latter holds a sufficient quantity of the former's voting securities.

subsidy: State assistance, in the form of money, for an industry. The purpose of a subsidy is to keep down the price of a commodity or service, i.e. maintain a level of demand sufficient to prevent a decline in the activity of the industry.

subsistence: That amount which is just sufficient to maintain a bare livelihood for a worker and his family.

supply: The supply of an economic good is the amount of it that is offered for sale at a particular price and at a certain time. At different prices, it is likely that producers will offer different amounts. At a higher price at a certain time, there would be the prospect of a greater gain for the producers and they would seek to supply more, if possible. On the other hand, at a lower price, the gain would be less, and less might be offered in supply in order to reduce the risks involved.

Jacob W. Chikuhwa

supply and demand, law of: This states that the price of an economic good is determined by the interaction of supply and demand. If supply is greater than demand at any one time, the surplus will generate a downward pressure upon the price. And conversely, if demand is greater than supply, the scarcity will force prices up.

support: This is a general term for the assistance given to industry by government. In particular, it refers to the giving of a subsidy and the guaranteeing of prices. A "goateed price" or a "price guarantee" is one that is made up to a previously agreed level by a government "deficiency payment" on top of the market price obtained.

surety: A security, in the sense of being a legal safeguard against loss.

symbolic language: Also known as assembly language (see low-level language), it uses mnemonic symbols to represent instructions; must be translated to machine language before it can be executed by the computer.

system: A combination of elements, their attributes and their inter-relationships that are organised in the pursuit of some objective.

system flowchart: The group of symbols that represent the general information flow; focuses on inputs and outputs rather than on internal computer operations.

system library: A collection of files in which various parts of an operating system are stored.

system residence device: An auxiliary storage device (disk, tape, or drum) on which operating-system programs are stored and from which they are loaded into primary storage.

systems analysis: A detailed step-by-step investigation of a system for the purpose of determining what it does and how it can best do it. It determines the objectives of a processing system, its organisation and its procedures.

systems analysis report: A report given to top management after the systems analysis phase has been completed to report the findings of the systems study; includes a statement of objectives, constraints, and possible alternatives.

systems analyst: The person who is the communication link or interface between users and technical persons (such as computer programmers and operators); responsible for systems analysis, design, and implementation of computer-based information systems.

systems design: The specification of the working relations between all the parts of a system in terms of their characteristic actions.

systems design report: A report given to top management after the systems analysis phase that explains how various designs will satisfy the information requirements; includes flowcharts, narratives, resources required to implement alternatives, and recommendations.

systems program: A sequence of instructions written to co-ordinate the operation of all computer circuitry and to help the computer run quickly and efficiently.

systems programmer: A programmer responsible for writing and maintaining systems software. See also programmer.

systems programming: The development of programs which form operating systems for computers.

TTTT

take-over bid: A take-over bid or offer is an offer made to shareholders of a company to buy their securities at a named price with the object of securing control of their company. A take-over bid is also called an offer to purchase.

tangible asset: Asset which can be physically identified or touched. Sometimes means only those assets which have a definite value, i.e. excludes intangible assets, goodwill and R&D expenditures carried forward.

tariff: A schedule of charges for goods or services. But, more commonly, a system of duties imposed on goods imported or exported either for revenue purposes or for protection or both.

taxation: A compulsory contribution to be made to the government. Taxation can be direct or indirect. Direct taxation is imposed immediately on the person or body who is intended to pay it and such taxes are levied upon income and capital, e.g. income tax, surtax, profits tax, death duty, stamps duty, etc. Indirect taxes, on the other hand, are borne ultimately by consumers when they buy goods and services, but they are paid initially by importers, producers, wholesalers, etc. Purchase taxes and customs duties are the main examples.

Jacob W. Chikuhwa

tax avoidance: The use of legally permissible methods of avoiding the payment of tax, or refraining from taxable actions.

tax evasion: The use of illegal methods to avoid payment of tax; also called "tax dodging".

tax exemption: A legally prescribed freedom from tax.

technology: Practical or industrial art(s); ethnological study of development of such arts; application of science.

telecommunication: The combined use of communication facilities, such as telephone systems and data-processing equipment.

telegraphic transfer: A technique of sending money from one place to another by a telegraphed instruction from one bank to another, often in a different country.

terminals: Input/output devices that are hooked into a communication network.

terms of trade: A comparison of a country's imports and exports in terms of their prices. Thus, iF the prices of imports rise relatively to the prices of exports, then the terms of trade have become less favourable; and vice versa. Terms of trade are usually measured by an index number computed from the import and export price indices: Index of Export Prices divided by Index of Import Prices, multiplied by 100, so that a fall in the index would indicate an adverse movement.

test data: A set of made-up or actual data used to test the correctness of a computer program.

testing: The process of determining whether the program satisfies its requirements.

text-editing: The process of using a word processor to enter and store a text file in the computer's secondary storage and then retrieve it for editing and storing as the old file, or as a new file.

ticket: A memorandum used in the Stock Exchange to inform the sellers of securities the names of buyers for the purpose of settlement.

time series: The measurement of changes that occur in a series of data over a period of time.

time sharing: An arrangement in which two or more users can access the same central computer system and receive what seem to be simultaneous results.

time sharing system: A central computer that can be used by various users at the same time for diverse tasks.

trade creditor: Account payable. Money owed for credit purchase. Current liability.

trade cycle: The trade, or business cycle is a general fluctuation in the economic activity of a society, where the means of production are mainly privately owned. The fluctuation is from a period of prosperity, or boom, down, through a recession, to depression, or slump, then a recovery to prosperity through a period known as revival. These fluctuations are characterised by expansions and contractions in most aspects of economic life, namely employment and unemployment, industrial production, earning and spending of wages and other incomes, the buying and selling of securities, domestic and foreign trade and prices.

trade discount: Deduction from the selling price of an invoice because the buyer is in the same trade as the seller. Not a cash discount.

trade investment: Investment in shares or debentures of another company in the same trade or industry. Long-term investment. Not a marketable security. Other asset in the balance sheet. Valued at cost, unless there is a substantial loss.

trade union: Organised association of workmen of a trade or group of allied trades formed for protection of their common interests.

trading stamps: A trading stamp is a document given by the retailer to the consumer at the time a purchase is made, representing the value of the purchase. Subsequently, these stamps can be exchanged for goods or money.

transaction: Change in two items in the balance sheet. Cash or credit transaction. May be sale, purchase, cash receipt, cash payment or accounting adjustment. Translated into debits and credits in the book-keeping records.

transaction file: A file containing data pertaining to a related set of business transactions to be processed in combination with a master file. For example, in a billing application, a transaction file of credit sales might be processed with a master file containing customer name, amount owed, etc.

Jacob W. Chikuhwa

transfer deed: The legal document which records the transfer of ownership of securities.

transfer earnings: Payments made by the State in the form of pensions, unemployment benefits, family allowances, national assistance, interest on the national debt, students' grants, etc., in return for which there is no productive contribution to the flow of goods and services. Collections are made from the incomes of others by taxation and then transferred, out of government revenue, to the income recipient.

transit field: The section of a cheque, pre-printed with magnetic ink, that includes the bank number.

trend: A detectable long-term movement in a time series.

trust: An arrangement whereby property is handed to or vested in a person or organisation to use or dispose of for the benefit of another person or organisation. In the business field, this has been adapted to mean an arrangement for the control of several firms to be under one direction, i.e. a trade combination for the purpose of obtaining monopoly powers.

trustee: (a) Person who holds property in trust for another (the Public Trustee — state official executing wills and trusts when invited); each of a body of persons, often elective, managing affairs of an institution. (b) State made responsible for government of an area; one who is responsible for preservation and administration of a thing.

turnover: The total amount of money changing hands in a business in a certain period of time, i.e. it is the total receipts in a day, week, month, etc. The turnover signifies the rate at which goods are being sold and is, therefore, measurable, in terms of the length of time that goods remain unsold.

UUUU

uncertainty: Limitation of accounting. Uncertainty at the end of each accounting period makes it difficult to determine the "true and fair" position. Uncertainty arises from: (a) incomplete transactions; (b) market value of inventory; (c) working life of fixed assets for depreciation calculations; (d) realisable values of current assets; (e) contingent liabilities not yet known or calculable.

underwriter: An insurer; one who gives his name to an insurance policy as guarantee of payments in the event of accident, loss, etc.

UNDO: A word-processing feature that allows the user to recover text that has been accidentally deleted.

unemployment: The state of being available for use in production, but not actually being in use. Unemployment is most commonly used in connection with labour.

update: In data processing, to change a record in a master file to reflect current transactions or changes. For example, to increase the amount owed in the accounts receivable record for a customer who makes a credit purchase.

USB: A USB flash drive consists of a flash memory data storage device integrated with a USB (Universal Serial Bus) interface. USB flash drives are typically removable and rewritable, and physically much smaller than a floppy disk.

user: Anyone who utilises a computer for problem solving or data manipulation.

user friendly: An easy-to-use, understandable software design that makes it easy for non-computer personnel to use an application software package.

usury: The charging of an excessive rate of interest on a loan, or any rate in excess of that legally permissible.

utility: (a) The power, or ability, to satisfy a human want. (b) A generalised routine for performing a specific data processing function in an efficient way.

utility routines: Also known as utility programs. Software used to perform some frequently required process in the operation of a computer system.

VVVV

value: (a) Accounting value — value according to accounting concepts, appropriate to the particular asset. Fixed assets at cost less depreciation. Current assets generally valued at cost or lower realisable value. (b) Market value — realisable value of inventory in the normal course of business (not in liquidation). (c) Real value — not known in accounting. (d) Use value — the power to satisfy human wants.

Jacob W. Chikuhwa

value added: This is the contribution made by a firm, involved with others in the production of a good or service, to the value of that good or service, i.e. the cost of materials, or the cost of the semi-finished good as purchased from another firm, is deducted from the market price of the good when it leaves a given enterprise.

value add tax: VAT is tax on amount by which value of an article has been increased at each stage of its production.

variable: A quantitative measurement to which a numerical value can be given, e.g. weight, or income.

variable costs: Also known as prime, running costs, they consist of payments for materials to be used in production, for power and for labour to be employed. These costs, therefore, increase as production increases and will only be constant when production is constant. Variable costs are to be viewed in comparison to fixed, or overhead, or supplementary or sunk costs which are incurred before actual production is possible and when it has stopped. These fixed costs are regular, established, unavoidable charges, e.g. taxes, rents, interest, insurance, maintenance and depreciation charges, reserves, certain salaries, etc.

variable proportions, law of: The law of diminishing returns deals with variations in the proportions of factors of production used by a firm. The law of variable proportions, or proportionality, is another expression of the principle. It implies that at any time, for any firm, there must be an ideal set of proportions, i.e. one which will yield optimum returns.

variables: Meaningful names assigned by the programmer to storage locations.

variance: See standard deviation.

vendor finance: This is a form of lending in which a company lends money to be used by the borrower to buy the vendor's products or property. Vendor finance is usually in the form of deferred loans from, or shares subscribed by, the vendor. The vendor often takes shares in the borrowing company. This category of finance is generally used where the vendor's expectation of the value of the business is higher than that of the borrower's bankers, and usually at a higher interest rate than would be offered elsewhere.

venture capital: Venture, or risk, capital that is subject to considerable risk, e.g. money capital invested in a new enterprise. Venture capital is sometimes used to describe ordinary shares.

verify: To check the accuracy and completeness of data.

visual display terminal: Also known as visual display unity (VDU). A terminal capable of receiving output on a cathode-ray tube (CRT) and, with special provisions, is capable of transmitting data through a keyboard.

value of credit: The total amount of bank credit that exists at a given time in a given economy.

WWWW

wage-price spiral: This is the name sometimes given to the alternation of successful wage demands and raises in the level of prices. See inflation.

wages: The reward paid to the factor of labour. The payment made to workers for placing their skills and energy at the disposal of an employer, the method of use of that skill and energy being at the employer's discretion and the amount of payment being in accordance with terms stipulated in a contract of service. Wages are paid in two main ways: by time, and by piece. (See incentive and piecework.)

wages policy: A wage policy means a comprehensive plan or system whereby wages are established and regulated; incomes policy has a wider connotation, denoting an attitude towards all kinds of income (interest, dividends, rent, etc.) In the Netherlands, for instance, wages policy means centralised legal regulation of wages; in Australia it is a system of compulsory arbitration; and in Sweden, it means the centralised negotiation of wage rates between employers and trade union organisations.

wasting asset: An irreplaceable asset, the life of which cannot be prolonged, e.g. mine.

watering stock: The act of making an issue of securities in excess of the company's real worth, i.e. an extent unwarranted by the company's assets.

waybill: A receipt which shows the goods being shipped.

Jacob W. Chikuhwa

wealth: Wealth, like value, can have several different meanings. In everyday speech, it usually means an abundance of material possessions, i.e. a stock of goods possessing utility and transferability and limited in quantity.

welfare: The economic well-being of the individual and the community. The economic welfare of the community as a whole is sometimes called its social welfare, to be distinguished from general and private welfare.

welfare economics: Welfare economics is concerned with the social consequences of economic behaviour which are capable of being measured objectively and handled in economic theory. The technique of welfare economics is to work out the effect of certain causes on the size and distribution of the national income. Welfare economics concentrates on aspects of the economy such as the presence of very rich and very poor, monopoly, and the lack of mobility of resources. It is concerned, therefore, with an evaluation of how far an economy is achieving maximum welfare and how its performance, in this respect, might be improved.

welfare state: A welfare state is established when government activity goes beyond the provision of the essential services of external defence, relief of dire poverty, law and order, and justice, to the provision of social services in order to increase the economic and social welfare of the community. This involves the establishment of public social services such as national or public assistance schemes, social insurance, family allowances and other services providing pensions and grants; health, education and other public services providing benefits in the form of goods or services; and a subsidy on housing, food, school meals and milk, and welfare foods.

wholesaler: As consumer goods flow regularly out of producing units and tend to be bought irregularly from retailers, a "buffer" function has to be performed between production and consumption. This is the basic function of the wholesaler. He may be in business on his account, or he may be part of a big concern which manufactures, holds stocks and retails the goods.

word processing: A computer system designed to handle words and text as input and output, rather than to perform calculations on numeric values. It is a technique for electronically storing, editing and manipulating text using an electronic keyboard, computer and printer.

word processor: An application software package that performs text-editing functions.

working capital: Special meaning — current assets less current liabilities. Not the same as capital.

working capital statement: It is a statement expressing a firm's investments in short-term assets.

work in process: Inventory. Stock. Work partially completed. Valued at the lower of manufacturing cost or market value.

YYYY

yield: The yield or dividend price ratio, of a security, is what it actually earns, taking into account the normal value, market valuation, and the dividend or interest paid.

ZZZZ

zero-base budgeting: A budgeting concept whereby all budget requests should be justified in detail from scratch (zero) each year departmental managers present their annual budgets.

BIBLIOGRAPHY

PART ONE

Applied Production and Operations Management, by J. Evans, D. Anderson, D. Sweeney, T. Williams, 1984, St. Paul.

Basic Small Business Management, by C. Baumback, 1983, Englewood, Cliffs, N.J.

Executive Guide to High-Impact Talent Management: Powerful Tools for Leveraging a Changing Workforce, The, by David DeLong and Steve Trautman, 2010.

Innovation and Entrepreneurship, by Peter F. Drucker, 1985, Forum.

Leader, The, A New Face for American Management, by M. Maccoby, 1981, Simon & Schuster, N.Y.

L. E. T. Leader Effectiveness Training, by T. Gordon, 1984, Tryck Centraltryckeriet AB, Borås.

Management, Tasks, Responsibilities, Practices, by Peter F. Drucker, 1975, LiberTryck, Stockholm.

Manpower Development Planning: Theory and an African Case Study (The Making of Modern Africa), by Berhanu Abegaz, 1994.

Modern Administration, by Peter Gorpe, 1981, Berlings, Arlöv.

One Page Talent Management: Eliminating Complexity, Adding Value, by Marc Effron and Miriam Ort, 2010.

Organisational Behaviour, Understanding and Prediction, by H. R. Bobbitt, Jr., R. H. Breinholt, R. H. Doktor, J. P. McNaul, 1978, Prentice-Hall, Inc.

Organisation and Environment, by P. Lawrence, J. Lorsh, 1967, Homewood, Ill.

Organisation Development, by W. L. French, C. H. Bell, Jr., 1973, Prentice-Hall, Inc., N. J.

Quality Circles, Changing Images of People at Work, by W. L. Mohr, H. Mohr, 1983, Addison-Wesley publishing Company, Inc.

Thriving on Chaos, by T. Peters, 1991, Excel/A California Limited Partnership.

Up the Organisation: How to Stop the Corporation from Stifling People and Strangling Profits, 2007, by Robert C. Townsend, Greenwhich, Com: Fawcell Publications.

PART TWO

Accounting Flows: Income, Funds, and Cash, by R. K. Jeedicke, R. T. Sprouce, 1965, Prentice-Hall, Inc. Englewood, Cliffs, N. J.

Analysis and Interpretation of Financial Statements, by Professor J. Langhout, 1984, South African Universities Press, Cape Town.

Audit Approach to Computers, An, by B. Jenkins & A. Pinkney, 1978, Cooper & Lybrand.

Business Administration in South Africa, by O. Britzius, 1982, Juta & Company Limited, Cape Town.

Corporate Strategy, by H. Ansoff, 1965, Hammordsworth.

Finance and Accounts for Managers, by D. Goch, 1981, Cox & Wyman Ltd., Reading.

Financial Intelligence: A Manager's Guide to Knowing What the Numbers Really Mean, by Karen Berman, Joe Knight and John Case, 2006.

Financial Management, by M. G. Wright, McGraw-Hill Inc., US; 2nd edition, 1980.

Financial Management (Barron's Business Library) by Jae K. Shim Ph.D. and Joel G. Siegel Ph.D., 2008.

Financial Management: Core Concepts, by Raymond Brooks, 2009.

Financial Management: Principles and Applications (11th Edition), by Sheridan Titman, John D. Martin, and Arthur J. Keown, 2010.

Financial Management: Theory & Practice, by Eugene F. Brigham and Michael C. Ehrhardt, 2010.

Financial Planning for Managers, by A. H. Taylor and R. E. Palmer, 1980, Cox & Wyman Ltd., Reading.

Fundamentals of Financial Management, by Eugene F. Brigham and Joel F. Houston, 2009

Fundamentals of Financial Management, by J. C. Van Horne and John Wachowicz, 11th Edition.

Growth, Profitability & Valuation, by A. Singh, G. Whittington, 1968, Cambridge.

Investment Decisions and Capital Costs, by J. T. S. Porterfield, 1965, Prentice-Hall, Inc. Englewood Cliffs, N. J.

Management of Business Finance, The, by J. Freear.

Jacob W. Chikuhwa

Management of Working Capital, The, by J. C. Burton, 1964, Prentice-Hall, Inc., Englewood Cliffs, N. J.
Managerial Economics, by J. Dean, 1951, Prentice-Hall, Inc.
Modern Managerial Finance, by J. R. Franks and J. E. Broyles, 1979.
Principles of Managerial Finance, Brief, by Lawrence J. Gitman, (5th Edition), 2008.
Profit in Small Firms, by T. D. Anderson, 1987, Avebury, Gower Publishing Company Limited, England, USA.
Theory and Measurement of Business, The, by E. Edwards, P. Bell, 1972, Los Angeles.
Theory of Profits, A, by A. Wood, 1975, Cambridge.

PART THREE
Art of Computer Programming, The, by D. Knuth, 1969, Reading, Ma.
Business Computers: Planning, Selecting and Implementing Your First Computer System, by Kein, Charles E. Merrill.
Business Data Systems, by H. D. Clifton, 1986, Prentice-Hall, International.
Business Systems, by R. G. Anderson, MacDonald & Evans, Plymouth.
Case Studies in Systems Design, by R. G. Anderson, MacDonald & Evans, Plymouth.
Charm of a List: From the Sumerians to Computerised Data Processing, The, by Lucie Dolezalova, 2009.
Computerised Book-keeping: An Accredited Textbook of the Institute of Certified Bookkeepers, by Dr. Peter Marshall, 2010.
Computers and Information Processing, by D. D. Spencer, 1985, Charles E. Merrill Publishing Company.
Concepts of Database Management, by Philip J. Pratt and Joseph J. Adamski, 2007.
Contemporary Database Marketing: Concepts and Applications, by Martin Baier, Kurtis M. Ruf, and Goutam Charkraborty, 2001.
Database Concepts (5th Edition) by David Krenke and David Auer, 2010.
Data Processing, by R. G. Anderson, 1974, MacDonald & Evans, Plymouth.
Data processing: An Introduction, by D. D. Spencer, Charles E. Merrill.

Bibliography

Data Quality: Concepts, Methodologies and Techniques (Data-Centric Systems and Applications), by Carlo Batini and Monica Scannapieco, 2010.

Effective Information Systems Management, by Thierauf and Reynolds, Charles E. Merrill.

Effective Management Information Systems: Accent on Current Practices, by Thierauf, Charles E. Merrill.

Introduction to Information Processing, by D. D. Spencer, Charles E. Merrill.

Mathematical Thinking in the Social Sciences, by P. Lazarsfeld, 1954, Glencoe, Ill.

Principles of Information Processing, by D. D. Spencer, Charles E. Merrill.

Quantitative Approaches in Business Studies, by C. Morris, 1983, MacDonald & Evans, Plymouth.

Statistics Without Tears, A Primer for No-mathematicians, by D. Rowntrel, 1985, Richard Clay (The Chaucer Press) Ltd., Bungay, Suffolk.

Theory of Games and Economic Behaviour, by J. von Neuman, O. Morgenstern, 1947, Princeton.

INDEX